WHAT
EISENHOWER
THINKS

Edited and Interpreted by
Allan Taylor

New York
THOMAS Y. CROWELL COMPANY

E
745
E35
A53

32321

Preface

What Dwight Eisenhower thinks is of tremendous importance to Americans in the critical year 1952. As this is written, it seems quite likely that General Eisenhower, despite his lack of political ambition, may become the next President of the United States by the demand of a majority of the nation's citizens. His popularity is an extraordinary tribute. It reflects a spontaneous trust, amid confusion and peril, in the strength, integrity, common sense and ability of a man who believes in the American people and who has shown his capacity to deal with threats to his country's heritage.

This faith is all the more impressive because much of it is instinctive rather than the result of accurate knowledge of the General's views. For Eisenhower, through force of circumstances, has been a political question mark. The reason lies in his sense of duty. He holds the sound conviction that a soldier of the Republic on active service should remain aloof from politics and domestic partisanship.

He has now stated his party preference. But he has also indicated that he will remain silent on other political subjects until there comes the "clear-cut call to political duty" that "would transcend" his responsibilities in Europe. One immediate reaction to this was an evident desire by many to know more about where Eisenhower stands.

Fortunately, much light is thrown on the matter by a study of the General's words. Although he has avoided political controversy, he has outlined his views of his nation and its place in the world in many addresses and statements during the past seven years. He has been vocal on both national and international problems. His ideas, it is true, were often expressed in general terms, but the inference as to how he would act on specific questions is usually plain. From the wealth of material one may learn not only his views on foreign policy, but his less publicized views on numerous domestic issues.

The purpose of this book is to present through Eisenhower's words—selected for their bearing on particular topics—his attitude toward some of the most vital problems confronting this nation today. It does not pretend to be a complete picture of the Eisenhower mind; it is based entirely on the thoughts that he has put on the public record. Some necessary biographical background has been added. The result, it is hoped, may help the reader to understand more clearly the kind of leadership to be expected from Dwight Eisenhower.

ACKNOWLEDGMENTS

The compilation of this book has been made possible by the helpful cooperation of numerous individuals and organizations. To all of these the compiler is deeply grateful. Leading the list is General Dwight Eisenhower himself, the unwitting coauthor, whose quoted words are the basis for this effort to explain his thinking.

Essential to the completed product were the ideas and the editorial advice of William Poole, Editor at Thomas Y. Crowell Company. Invaluable help was given by Mr. John Hastings, Acting Director, Public Information Office at Columbia University, who made available the texts of addresses delivered by General Eisenhower during the period when he was the active head of Columbia University. Thanks are also due to the unequaled files of *The New York Times,* which were drawn upon for the text of several speeches and many of the quotations needed to round out the Eisenhower record.

The compiler also would like to acknowledge his debt to several biographies, among them Kenneth S. Davis' *Soldier of Democracy,* which gives a valuable insight into Eisenhower the person; Francis Trevelyan Miller's biography, *Eisenhower, Man and Soldier,* and *General Ike,* by Alden Hatch. General Eisenhower's *Crusade in Europe* and *My Three Years with Eisenhower,* by the General's former naval aide, Harry Butcher, have also furnished useful background.

For the rest, the editor is grateful to various individuals and organizations for material furnished. Among them are: The Wings Club, Inc.; The Economic Club of New York; Guy Emery Shipler, Editor, *The Churchman;* A. M. Powell, Director of Publicity, Lafayette College; The Congress of Industrial Organizations; Mrs. Ruth Hughes of the Department of State; The Association of National Advertisers, Inc.; E. S. Wilson of Amherst College; Raymond A. McConnell, Jr., Editor, *The Nebraska State Journal,* Lincoln, Nebraska; Arthur J. Goldsmith, of New York, who supplied valuable information; and Miss Ellen Kuhn of the Montclair Public Library. Finally, the writer's deepest gratitude is given to his wife, without whose help and forbearance this effort would not have been completed.

Contents

PART I

The Eisenhower Story

CHAPTER I

Youthful Years

How a man thinks and acts are determined by many factors, not the least among them his childhood background and training. Inheritance enters in, and so do adult experiences, but the formative years, the setting into which he was born and where he received his first sharp impressions of life, are likely to color all the man's subsequent reactions to life. For this reason it is important to look briefly at the beginnings of the Eisenhower record.

The story of Ike Eisenhower is the perfect American success story. It typifies the chronicle, so fascinating to the American mind, of the self-made man. Basically, it is the story that Horatio Alger told so many times under so many titles (and so contributed his part to the American creed)—of the boy who rose, by reason of sound character, intelligence, courage and hard work, from humble beginnings to high position and great honors, and did it without losing his fundamental virtues of simplicity and integrity. If the Eisenhower real life version lacks some of the more melodramatic elements of the Alger rags-to-riches formula, it contains most of the others, including a great deal of pluck and even some luck.

Dwight David Eisenhower was not born in a log cabin, that supposedly nineteenth-century prerequisite to political success. But he didn't miss it by much. Indeed, the modest frame dwelling near the railroad tracks in Denison, Texas, where the event took place on October 14, 1890, was virtually the small town equivalent, at the time, of the earlier frontiersman's log cabin. Moreover, the family was, as the phrase went, in straitened circumstances. Dwight was the third son. His father, David, who had studied engineering, was working as a mechanic, or according to some accounts, as a stationary engineer, for the Cotton Belt Railroad and was making less than $40 a month. Even in 1890 the sum was barely sufficient to feed and clothe five people.

How the Eisenhowers of Kansas, who were rather substantial folk, came to be in Denison in this low state of fortune is a question that calls for a short excursion into family history.

The Eisenhowers were solid, deeply religious Pennsylvania "Dutch" who had come out to Kansas in 1878. Their ancestral home had been the German Palatinate. The name was originally Eisenhauer, meaning "iron striker" or "iron beater"— which in family legend connoted a warrior strain. If so, the strain was remote. During the Reformation the Eisenhauers joined one of the Mennonite sects, whose beliefs included a strong opposition to militarism and war. To escape religious persecution during the savage Thirty Years War from 1618 to 1648, the Eisenhauers moved to Switzerland, where they remained for about a century. Then they are believed to have resided briefly in Holland and to have emigrated to "Penn's Woods" about 1732. They settled near the Susquehanna.

Like others around them of similar heritage and persuasion, they were industrious and skillful farmers who conserved the soil and grew bounteous crops. By custom and tenet most of the Pennsylvania "Dutch" were peaceful people, sober in habits and dress, who frowned on extravagance, "show" and worldly excesses of all kinds. Nevertheless, they admired those who prospered. Although they deplored vanities, they highly valued the institution of private property and they sought to acquire property by thrift, work and ofttimes by making sensible marriages. Scrupulously honest, they were shrewd bargainers who provided well and ate well. On Sundays they gathered to hear their preachers and to consult their consciences.

They were accustomed to cooperative effort for the common good, especially in social and political ways. Some of

2

the Eisenhowers, incidentally, deviated from pacifism; they fought in both the Revolution and the Civil War. Their faith made these people rebels against imposed authority, particularly of the ecclesiastical kind. But—and this is a fact that should be remembered about the Eisenhower background—in most respects they were thoroughly conservative.

The future General's grandfather, Jacob, had bookish leanings which led him into the ministry without, however, interfering with his farming or his acquisition of worldly goods. He was a leader of the Brethren in Christ, generally known as the River Brethren because they lived along the Susquehanna. He built a comfortable two-story brick house which still stands in Elizabethville, Pennsylvania. Sunday services were held in the parlor.

The post–Civil War urge to seek new opportunities in the West was felt in steady-going Pennsylvania as elsewhere throughout the East. The Brethren discussed the matter, finally sent some of their members to investigate Kansas. The mission returned with praise of the land around a town called Abilene. So a considerable number of the Brethren from Pennsylvania and Maryland decided to move. Jacob and his family joined the expedition. Jacob's son David was then fifteen years old.

This community effort appears to have been well organized and financed. The colony settled around Abilene in the valley of the Kansas River and soon began to prosper. In time Jacob acquired enough wealth to start all of his children off with a farm of their own.

David, however, lacked the family interest in farming. His bent was toward machinery. He wanted to become an engineer. At the age of twenty he persuaded his father to send him to a small college called Lane University, at Lecompton, Kansas. It was here that he met and fell in love with the girl who was to become his wife.

Her name was Ida Elizabeth Stover. She was vivacious, energetic, charming, popular. The attraction was mutual. Before the end of his second year at Lane, David Eisenhower reached the conclusion that it was more important to marry this girl than to finish college. He proposed and was accepted.

There came the question of how to make a living. David

3

still didn't want to farm. He decided to go into partnership in a general merchandise business. To finance the venture he mortgaged, with Jacob's consent, the farm Jacob gave him. His partner was a young man named Good, and the site of the business was a small village south of Abilene named Hope. Ida Stover and David Eisenhower were married on September 23, 1885.

For a year or so things seemed to go well. But David was no businessman. He trusted too many people. Neither partner, apparently, paid sufficient attention to the ledgers. David's Good Hope proved to be a mirage. Creditors presented demands which collections could not meet. In 1888 came disaster. The store was sold, the farm mortgage was foreclosed, and David, who had one son, with a second on the way, left Abilene to take the first job he could get—one in the railroad shops in Denison. Ida strove to salvage what she could, which was little. After the birth of her second son she joined David in Texas.

If the advent of Dwight, the third of the sons, coincided with a low ebb in the family fortunes, happier, though not much more prosperous, times were ahead. One of the successful enterprises which the Brethren had established in Abilene was a creamery. The foreman was Chris Musser, who had married David's siser, Amanda. Jacob Eisenhower wanted his son back home in Abilene; he turned to his son-in-law for help. Chris offered David a job running the machinery of the creamery. David accepted. Thus, only a few months after Dwight's birth, the Eisenhowers—father, mother, sons Arthur and Edgar, and baby Dwight—settled in Abilene, Kansas.

In Abilene three other sons were to be born and raised to manhood (another died in infancy). The six brothers, each different and yet each alike, were to form an unusually closely-knit fraternity. All, in their different ways, were to achieve success. For that and for the qualities which helped them succeed, they owed a great debt to the staunch character, the cheerful industry, the daily training, the ever-present wisdom, and the expert management of their mother. She was typical of the courageous, understanding and capable homemakers who had held families together on the frontier and who inculcated the basic virtues into generations

4

of Americans. She exemplified the best in American family life. She was a remarkable woman.

Ida Stover came of people similar in many respects to the Eisenhowers. Research by Eisenhower biographers indicates that the Stovers emigrated to America from Switzerland, where they had also been religious refugees from Germany, about the same time as the Eisenhowers. They landed in Virginia and pushed westward across the Blue Ridge to settle in the Shenandoah Valley, then the frontier.

Ida Elizabeth was born in Augusta County, Virginia, in 1862, at the time Stonewall Jackson was conducting in that same area his brilliant Valley campaigns. The Stovers were anti-slavery and their religious faith gave them, like the Eisenhowers, an antipathy to war. Nevertheless, they suffered from war's ravages during the next three years as the armies fought up and down the Shenandoah. Hearing of these things later, Ida Stover hated war. Her mother died when she was very young and, as there were many children, she was sent to live with an uncle, who became her guardian on her father's death.

While she was still a small child two of her brothers went out to Kansas. She resolved to follow them when she could. She had to wait until she was twenty-one and could receive her small inheritance. With it, in 1883 she went to Topeka in company with relatives and, being ambitious for an education, soon enrolled in the college at Lecompton.

The early life of Dwight Eisenhower and his brothers was rugged if judged by current ideas of how to raise children and by present American standards of comfort. But the children apparently did not realize this. Theirs was a busy, practical, and, from all the evidence, a happy upbringing.

The first house in Abilene was small, too cramped for the growing family. Ida Eisenhower was delighted when, some years later, the opportunity came to move into a larger house on the outskirts of town. It had a barn where the children could play and there was enough land around it to raise fruits and vegetables for the family table and to provide a surplus for sale to more prosperous Abilenites. As the children grew old enough, they went to school and on Sundays attended the

Sunday school at the meeting house of the Brethren, where they did not particularly distinguish themselves for piety.

On Sundays as well as week days they had their allotted chores. They helped by milking the cow, by bringing in firewood, by planting and weeding the garden and, in time, by selling garden truck around the town.

Under their mother's efficient management they were taught to do the job that was needed and to do it quickly and well. If it wasn't done well, they were sent back to do it again. There were occasions when the rod was not spared. The boys learned that rewards must be earned, that nothing is gained without effort. But when the job was done they could play. Mother Eisenhower's system worked so well that, despite the number of duties the children had, there was nearly always time for play.

Sometimes chores and play were intermingled, with strange results. One of the family stories concerns the time Dwight and his older brother Edgar, who fought bitterly but joined forces against outsiders, were assigned the duty of making pie crust while their parents were at church. They made the dough, kneaded it, and then were struck by the possibilities of using the lump as a ball to be thrown and caught between them. The game went well for a time, but then one of the brothers missed and the dough fell on the kitchen floor. There were subsequent misses, and with each one the dough grew dirtier and grayer. Finally one of the contestants spied the parents in the offing. The dough was hastily rolled out and put in the oven. At dinner Mother Eisenhower remarked that the pie crust was a good job, though it seemed a little tougher than usual. Neither boy dared confess until years later.

Edgar and Dwight had homeric battles. Edgar, the larger, usually won, sometimes getting Dwight down and pounding his head against the floor. But Dwight was always ready for another round. Mother Eisenhower accepted the fights with equanimity. She seldom interfered. She understood that the boys were working off their physical energies as well as their petty grievances against each other. She was untroubled by the possibility of lasting damage, physical or psychic.

Dwight had a temper and he early proved his physical

courage in an environment which greatly admired that quality. Perhaps his most famous battle was with a school-mate who had been accustomed to lording it over the class and to beating down all opposition. The two met by appointment after school. Ringed by adult and small fry spectators, they fought to a long and staggering draw, each bloody but unbowed. As a result of the bout they became good friends.

The family had its ups and downs, the children their trials and times of danger. There was the day when Milton, the youngest of the brothers, was stricken with scarlet fever, then a much more deadly disease than now. For six weeks the de-voted Ida Eisenhower was quarantined in the sickroom while she struggled to save her son's life, and David and the older boys cooked the meals.

There was also the time Dwight skinned his knee and de-veloped blood poisoning. He did not realize the danger of the infection until his leg was badly swollen. The family doc-tor examined him, shook his head and advised amputation.

Dwight said no; he would rather die. The doctor warned that the longer they waited the more of the leg he would have to take off, and that if the poison reached the pelvis it would mean death. The parents could not decide. The fever and agony mounted. But Dwight was adamant. He realized that he would "go out of his head" and feared that in delirium he could not prevent the operation. So he ordered Edgar to stand guard. Convinced that his brother meant what he said, Edgar did sentry duty for two days and nights while the crisis came—and miraculously passed. Aided by great physical stamina, Dwight's recovery was rapid.

Courage of this sort, and the sense of values that preferred death to a lifelong physical handicap, were part of a com-munity background which in these formative years greatly influenced Dwight's character and thinking.

Abilene, only a few years before the Brethren had settled there, had been one of the toughest towns in the West. In the period from 1867, when the railroad reached Abilene, until 1872, when the cattle market shifted further west, the place had been the northern terminus of the famous 1000-mile-long Chisholm Trail. Up this trail from the ranges of Texas, which had become glutted with cattle during the Civil War, poured

7

millions of wild steers for the slaughterhouses of the prosperous North. The steers were herded by thousands of equally wild cowpunchers who, with money in their pockets, "cut loose" in Abilene. Gamblers flocked in to share the golden harvest. Saloons and bawdy houses flourished. Shootings were so commonplace they scarcely aroused interest.

After two years of such doings the decent elements of Abilene joined forces to impose law and order. A succession of cold-eyed, quick-shooting characters—Wild Bill Hickok was the most famous of them—were hired as town marshals to clean up the place. Eventually they succeeded, though not without casualties in their own ranks.

This wild and woolly past—not so far back in time when Ike Eisenhower and his schoolmates were growing up in Abilene—had its effects on folkways. To the boys of Abilene, Hickok, Billy the Kid, and other desperadoes of the post–Civil War West were glamorous figures. A frontier version of cops and robbers was a favorite local game. To this day Ike Eisenhower when seeking relaxation likes to read, not the whodunits to which Woodrow Wilson and many other busy men have turned, but pulp magazine Westerns. During the war in off moments, he read Westerns by the bale.

The frontier traditions of Abilene did more than produce in the future General a liking for stereotyped Western fiction. They played a part in molding his characer and in determining his responses toward the deeper questions of existence.

On the one hand, they helped inculcate a pragmatic, will-it-work? approach to the major difficulties of life. People on the frontier had to be practical in the immediate sense. Their survival often depended upon arriving almost instantly at the correct answer to a suddenly imposed problem. They were individualists, and on their faith in themselves as individuals they stood or died. On the other hand, they could not afford or did not have the interest to indulge in metaphysical speculation or the fine balancing of philosophic theories as to how human affairs should be conducted.

As Kenneth S. Davis discerningly pointed out in his excellent biography of Eisenhower, the individualism of the frontiersman made him prize personal liberty above all else. He could join in community effort for tangible rewards and he usually abided by majority decisions, but he would not tolerate regimentation or dictatorship either by an individual or by a group. In a later frame of reference, he was unalterably opposed to both the Hitlers and the Politburos of this world.

He relied on his own judgment. His mental life was largely external, having to do with the means of achieving his own ends. He was not a doubter or a questioner; he was a go-getter. He was not a Hamlet; he was a man of action. He was the eternal optimist who believed in his ability to better himself and to control his destiny. He was the yea-sayer.

This, up to a point, was all to the good. But the frontiersman, in his pragmatic approach to life, was prone to overlook or was entirely unaware of some of the most subtle problems of human existence. To more sophisticated minds he was a primitive, certainly not a philosopher. There was a great deal that he didn't know about the world. In his view, ideas were generally valid only if they "worked." Although he had a strong sense of personal ethics, once matters got beyond personal relationships, the ends could often be made to justify the means.

Young Dwight Eisenhower absorbed this pragmatic attitude, as was shown on numerous future occasions to the benefit of the Free World. But he also acquired from his ancestral and boyhood background a compensating sense of justice, democracy and fair play which have blended the man of action and the man of thought into a leader who, if he does not always know the immediate answer, will approach the problem as one to be solved practically rather than on the basis of a preconceived theory, and will find the answer in terms of the common good and his own ethical precepts.

Of these future problems Dwight Eisenhower the schoolboy was in large part happily unaware. He went to high school, where he played football and baseball enthusiastically and expertly, showed a talent for leadership, and was by all accounts the sort of adolescent extrovert that one thinks of as the typical, healthy American boy. His organizing ability was shown when he helped form an athletic association to finance the buying of sports equipment and kept it alive against the disinterest of school authorities.

He was not "bookish" and he was not, at this period, a particularly outstanding student, though at his best he was good indeed. His grades ranged from average to excellent—from the low 80's to 95 or better. If he showed any particular aptitude it was for English; he was always able to express himself clearly and effectively, either orally or in writing. His high school record indicates that he was a good student whenever he made up his mind to work at it. It also indicates that he didn't always work at it as hard as he might have. But he showed even then an amazing ability to absorb facts which he considered interesting or useful.

During these high school years Dwight and some of his friends used to gather at the office of Joe Howe, the editor and owner of the weekly *Abilene News*. Howe was interested in boyish problems and was a recipient of boyish confidences; he also had a considerable collection of books. He apparently had a very stimulating effect on the budding mental life of the future General.

At this time Dwight also began to go to parties and date the girls, many of whom belonged to families of somewhat higher economic status than the Eisenhowers, as such distinctions went in small town society in the early years of the twentieth century. But Dwight had no class consciousness. If the difference in worldly goods affected him at all, it merely spurred him to work harder—and he was already working nights at the creamery as a helper. By some of the Abilene folk he was regarded as a rough diamond, well raised but perhaps a bit on the tough side. But he was universally liked, and several of the more thoughtful maidens of Abilene recognized in him a first rate intellect.

Dwight graduated from high school in 1909. There followed a period of indecision when he was not sure what course to follow, what to make of himself. He did hard physical labor, at the creamery and at odd jobs, and saved his money, part of which helped finance brother Edgar at college. He was vaguely dissatisfied with himself but the prospects for a higher education were not bright.

Then came the turning point which decided his career. One of his friends had long been ambitious to go to West Point. He had been unable to secure the appointment but had, instead, been offered an appointment by his Congressman to Annapolis. He urged Dwight to seek an Annapolis appointment, too. Dwight decided that here was the opportunity to further himself for which he had been waiting. He enlisted the help of influential friends and secured, through one of the Kansas Senators, Joseph L. Bristow, the chance to take a competitive examination that, if he passed, might open the way either to Annapolis or West Point. His parents, although they had no liking for a military career, offered no objection.

Dwight went to work. He borrowed books, he crammed. His capable mind absorbed in a few weeks a tremendous amount of information that would help in the test ahead. In the examination he stood second out of eight candidates. But then he learned that, at twenty, he was overage for an Annapolis entrance but not too old for West Point, which accepted candidates up to twenty-one. To the temporary regret of himself and his friend, he headed for West Point. Thus was taken the first step in the adult progress of Dwight Eisenhower.

CHAPTER II

Army Years

The military career of the future General of the Army Eisenhower began on June 14, 1911. On that summer day the young man from the plains of Kansas gained his first impressions of the stately citadel-like buildings of West Point where, amid the rugged grandeur of rocky headlands overlooking the Hudson, he was to spend the next four years of his life.

He went through the required "processing." He filled out forms, surrendered his civilian possessions and identity, was assigned to quarters and to a company, and took the oath of allegiance to support the Constitution and to "obey the legal orders of my superior officers and the rules and articles governing the Armies of the United States." He became one of the browbeaten "beasts," or plebes, whose endurance is tested during their first year at the Point by upperclassmen while other qualities are being gauged by the rigorous discipline and the demanding classroom standards of the Academy. But at the same time he became a member of a dedicated elite. He joined the famous Corps, of stern exactions and high traditions, which for 150 years has produced leaders whose lives were molded by the West Point motto: Duty, Honor, Country.

At West Point Cadet Eisenhower was in the upper third of his classes. He was not notably deficient in any subject, nor was he outstandingly brilliant as a student. In his first year he stood about the middle of the upper half of his class; when he graduated in 1915 he ranked 61st in a class of 164. Under the strict routine of West Point he appears to have collected more than his share of demerits—chiefly for such minor infractions of the rules as being late to formations or not keeping his room in meticulous order. He showed a genial talent for leadership; he formed many lasting friendships. At the

Academy "Ike"—a nickname dating from early school days and one which his mother never cared for—became well known and universally liked.

His outstanding achievements, however, were in athletics. His love of football, acquired in high school, made him work harder at the game than at his studies. In the fall of 1912 his performance was so good that Eastern sportswriters hailed him as one of the coming stars of the gridiron. He distinguished himself in the Carlisle game against the great Jim Thorpe. Then, in a game with Tufts, he suffered a knee injury that put him out for the rest of the season. This injury, with its subsequent complications, virtually ended his football career. Thereafter, he was forced to confine himself mainly to coaching—and to cheerleading.

All in all, Dwight Eisenhower's record at West Point showed the presence of some of the qualities which were later to figure in his amazing rise. But some of the other qualities, including the steady application of his fact-absorbent mind to his work, were yet to be developed. He was a better-than-average cadet, but few sensed in him the figure he was to become.

The first assignment of Second Lieutenant Eisenhower was to the 19th Infantry regiment at Fort Sam Houston, in San Antonio, Texas. The date was September 15, 1915. In Europe vast armies had been fighting for more than a year in the conflict that was to be termed World War I. At home, troubles with Mexico were soon to appear. The young lieutenant sensed the opportunities and obligations that lay ahead for army officers and began to apply to his job the knowledge he had gained at the Academy.

At the same time he fell in love. At the fort he met a charming and very popular girl from Denver, named Mamie Doud, whose parents customarily spent the winters in the mild climate of San Antonio. She was much sought after for dances and dates by the young officers of the post. Dwight, immediately smitten, set out to win her. There followed a determined courtship in which he used all his magnetism and persuasive powers. Years later Mamie was to recall that his conversation had fascinated her—and she added that it had continued to fascinate her ever since.

Dwight quickly fitted himself into the Doud family circle. He liked the Douds; the Douds liked him. Eventually the well-to-do Douds faced the fact that their daughter was seriously thinking of marrying a fine young man but one who followed an ill-paid profession in which, with the slow rate of promotion in the regular army, there seemed little personal future. If they were not enthusiastic about the prospect, they offered no objections. Dwight and Mamie were married in Denver on July 1, 1916. On the same day Dwight was promoted to first lieutenant.

Events were moving rapidly toward American entry into the European war. The army was being expanded, and Lieutenant Eisenhower was making a reputation as a capable instructor in training camps. In April, 1917, after Germany's adoption of unrestricted submarine warfare, Woodrow Wilson asked for a declaration of war against the Central European powers. In the following September Eisenhower was assigned as instructor at the officers training camp at Fort Oglethorpe, Georgia. In the same month was born the Eisenhowers' first son, Doud Dwight Eisenhower—whose death at the age of three was to be a tragic event in the lives of the parents. The young father was sent to various duties that led, in March, 1918, to his assignment as commander of Camp Colt, a tank-training center, at Gettysburg, Pennsylvania. He had risen to the rank of captain.

This assignment was to his liking. He was one of the early tank enthusiasts and saw in it possibilities for breaking the bloody stalemate in Europe. And it was at Camp Colt that Eisenhower's genius for organization and his ability to "make do" with little first came to the attention of the higher-ups in the army. He was in command of six thousand men and the facilities were inadequate to care for them. Moreover, he was supposed to train them in tank operations, but no tanks could be had from the tardy American production lines. Somehow he did it. The camp became one of the most efficient in the country. The training, even though theoretical, proved its value in the latter battles of the war. Eisenhower was made a major, then a lieutenant colonel (temporary). For his work at Camp Colt he received, ten years later, the Distinguished Service Medal.

14

But at the time a great disappointment awaited him. He grew restive under continued stateside duties. Many of his classmates were fighting in Europe. He asked for overseas assignment. The War Department was reluctant to transfer him from the job he was performing so well, but eventually the orders came through. He was to go overseas with a tank unit on November 18, 1918. On November 11 came the Armistice: it was over over there. Lieutenant Colonel Eisenhower's explosive comments may be imagined by the many veterans of World War I who were forced to fight the war at home.

There followed two decades of between-wars service and constant preparation for a future which at times seemed highly uncertain. After the expansion of the army in the war, the prospects for promotion in the shrinking peacetime regular army greatly diminished; it was not until 1920 that Eisenhower achieved the permanent rank of major which he had held on a temporary basis in 1918. Sixteen more years were to pass before he regained his Camp Colt rank of lieutenant colonel!

If the Eisenhower morale at times suffered, that did not interfere with work and with the enjoyment of the army friendships for which both Dwight and Mamie were so well fitted. Wherever they were stationed, the two made a home which became a center of happy social life and a gathering place for their many friends.

One of the friendships formed in the immediate postwar period while Ike was stationed at Camp Meade, Maryland, was that with George S. Patton, a tank commander in World War I whose abilities, coupled with his flair for the dramatic gesture, had already made him a legendary figure in army anecdote. (One story depicted Patton, a former cavalryman, as riding astride a tank waving a sword as he led an attack.) It may be ventured that Eisenhower and Patton did not have too much in common except drive, capability, and devotion to the army. Nonetheless, their friendship was a close one during the next twenty-five years as each served his country in his own way.

Patton, it appears, was instrumental in bringing together

his friend Ike and Brigadier General Fox Connor, one of the most able of American officers. Connor was a farseeing man who had already reached the conclusion from his own observations and his understanding of historical forces that World War I was merely the first phase in a long period of world conflict. His ideas impressed Eisenhower with the necessity for being ready for future tests; they gave him incentive to stay in the army and to learn as much as he could about the tasks of higher command. In turn the young tank specialist seemed to Connor to have the makings of one of the military leaders that his country would need in the dangerous years ahead.

Connor became commander of a brigade in the Panama Canal Zone and, needing a capable executive officer, wrote his young friend. In January, 1922, Major Eisenhower began a tour of duty in the Canal Zone that lasted until the autumn of 1924. He tightened up discipline and improved the performance of the brigade so well that he confirmed Connor's estimates of his qualities. It was during this Panama period that a second son, John Doud Eisenhower, was born to Mamie, who had gone back to Denver in preparation for the event.

Under Connor's guidance Eisenhower's already great interest in the reading of military history and theory was increased—as was his determination to be prepared for any future contingency. This determination is illustrated by the story that Eisenhower decided to have his appendix out when a good opportunity came—not that the appendix was bothering him, but just in case it should make trouble in a time of crisis. Back in the States he later had the operation for just that reason.

The space is lacking here to trace the whole step-by-step progress of the future General up the rungs of experience and specialized military knowledge that prepared him for the duties Connor had foreseen. But a few revealing—and perhaps decisive—steps should be noted.

After Panama Eisenhower served as a recruiting officer at Fort Logan, Colorado, and in the leisure the job gave him worked out problems that had been previously used at the

Command and General Staff School at Fort Leavenworth. He was ready when his appointment to the school came in the summer of 1925. During the year's course he studied as he had never studied before. The result: in May 1926 he graduated first in the class. Since leaving West Point, Ike Eisenhower had learned how to use his brilliant mind to full advantage.

Later that year he was offered an assignment to the American Battle Monuments Commission in Washington. This involved making a concise and well-organized guide book out of a mass of ill-sorted information about the American battlefields in France. He was already known as a writer of clear and meaningful English. He accepted.

His work won the commendation of General John J. Pershing and led—after a course at the Army War College—to an interval in Paris where he revised the guidebook on the basis of personal research. In the process he learned a great deal about the terrain and the roads of France that was to be of value fifteen years later. He returned to the United States on the eve of the Big Crash, in September, 1929.

Next he studied the American industrial component in the waging of war. He helped to found the Army Industrial College and learned about military-industrial problems from its speakers.

Then came an opportunity to help in drawing up reports and other official documents for General Douglas MacArthur, who had become Chief of Staff in 1930. For two years Eisenhower was in close contact with that great soldier, but politically controversial figure, who was to lead American arms to victory in a series of brilliant campaigns in the Pacific while his erstwhile aide was doing the same in Europe.

The association led MacArthur, when he became military adviser of the Commonwealth of the Philippines in 1935, to offer Eisenhower the place of assistant military adviser. Ike accepted.

He stayed in the Philippines for four years, occupied with various aspects of the defense of the islands. This meant working against time and against the handicap of insufficient resources. Eisenhower helped write the Commonwealth Defense Act, helped establish the Philippine Military Academy.

He was in charge of the organization of the fledgling Philippine Air Force and, flying about the islands on various tasks, decided to learn how to operate airplanes. He took lessons and became a pilot at an age considered rather advanced to learn flying.

The Philippine tour was terminated when he was ordered back to the United States in 1939. The indications are that Ike Eisenhower welcomed the change because of the shift in international affairs which took place. World War II had begun with Hitler's invasion of Poland. The focus was again on Europe rather than the Orient.

He reached San Francisco in January, 1940, served on various assignments, and in November of that year was made Chief of Staff of the Third Division. In March of 1941 he became Chief of Staff of the Ninth Army Corps at Fort Lewis, Washington, and in the same month was promoted to the rank of colonel (temporary). After thirty years in the army he had achieved the eagles of a "chicken colonel," which for so long had been his ambition.

But this was merely the beginning. Faced with world conflagration, the army was expanding and was toughening up. Eisenhower's work in Pacific Coast maneuvers led to his appointment, in June, 1941, as Chief of Staff of General Walter Kreuger's Third Army, with headquarters at familiar old Fort Sam in San Antonio. The Third Army soon took the field in the forests and swamps of Louisiana in the largest peacetime maneuvers the country had yet seen, involving 220,000 men. Opposed to the Third Army was the Second Army under General Ben Lear, which included a tank force led by George Patton.

At the end of the war games the Third Army was adjudged the winner, a result due in no small part to the effectiveness of Ike Eisenhower as Chief of Staff. He returned to Fort Sam Houston where, in September, he received the rank of brigadier general (temporary). The next and most dramatic stage of the Eisenhower career was shortly to begin.

CHAPTER III

Architect of Victory

That fateful day of history, December 7, 1941, brought to an abrupt end the uncertainties, the tensions, and the debates over foreign policy which had marked America's course through the first twenty-seven months of World War II. It also brought to a newly made and relatively obscure brigadier general of the American army—known to his friends as Ike— the opportunity of a lifetime, and with it the tremendous responsibilities for which his special talents and thirty years of hard work in his chosen profession had fitted him.

It was 7:55 of a bright morning in subtropical Hawaii when the first Japanese bombs fell on the ships and airfields of Pearl Harbor. In Washington, five thousand miles to the east, where Secretary of State Cordell Hull sat in his office awaiting Japan's reply to President Roosevelt's last-minute peace appeal—which was to be delivered by the emissaries Kurusu and Nomura—the time was 1:25 in the afternoon. At Fort Sam Houston, in San Antonio, the time was 12:25. Ike Eisenhower, who was weary from long hours of work for months past and who had completed an extra Sunday morning stint to clear his desk in anticipation of Christmas leave —had gone home for dinner and a nap, leaving orders that he was not to be disturbed. But he was.

He returned to his office and said quietly to his staff: "Well, boys, it's come." If he was surprised it was not at the fact of war, which he had expected, but at the manner of its coming. He tackled the myriad of detailed duties which the new situation brought to army officers all over the nation.

Five days later the new General received urgent orders to report to Washington for a staff assignment. He responded with heavy heart; it seemed that he was about to sit out another war at home, this time behind a desk. He had never commanded troops in battle. He was known as a "brain worker"; his recognized skills stemmed from the clarity of his thinking and writing and from his capacity to plan and coordinate complex military operations. If that meant a desk job, he must resign himself to it. With his customary sense of duty, he did.

At the capital he learned that he was to be Assistant Chief, under his old friend Brigadier General Leonard Gerow, of the important War Plans Division of the General Staff. His first assignment, ironically, was to the Pacific defenses. He had left the Philippines because he saw in Germany the primary enemy and was convinced that until Germany was beaten, Europe would be the main theater of war. But he plunged with typical energy into his job. This involved, among other things, the almost insoluble problem of arranging from Washington to get supplies to MacArthur's beleaguered forces on Bataan.

The selection of Eisenhower for this post, his first step toward fame, appears to have been due to his long-term record rather than to any specific exploit, or to friends at court. Although Connor and others with influence had spotted him for leadership, his acquaintance with Chief of Staff General George Marshall, head of the army hierarchy, had been quite casual. His work in the Louisiana maneuvers may or may not have influenced the decision. Asked about the matter later, he grinned in embarrassment and said he guessed "someone must have told the General I was a hot shot."

In any event, General Marshall at once began carefully to observe and weigh the new Assistant Chief of War Plans. Marshall soon found in Eisenhower a man who was not only extremely competent, but who also had the magnetic personality, the broad understanding of global strategy, and the calm and realistic confidence in ultimate success that were required for high command in the perilous times ahead.

Such leadership was badly needed. The immediate prospect was far from cheerful. The Japanese were sweeping unchecked through southeast Asia and the southern Pacific. In Russia the Nazi armies, though stopped short of Moscow, were deep in the country, and Hitler was confident of crushing the Red Army in the spring. Britain stood alone in the

West. Not for months could America's gathering strength have an appreciable effect on the struggle.

Yet in this dark period there was formed in Washington the beginning of a close partnership unparalleled in the history of war. British Prime Minister Winston Churchill and his Chiefs of Staff arrived to confer with President Roosevelt and his military planners. On January 2, 1942, the foundation of the United Nations organization was laid in a military alliance of twenty-six countries. The group known as the Combined Chiefs of Staff was set up to mesh Anglo-American and Allied strength. Priority was given to the war on Germany.

Dwight Eisenhower took part in a number of high-level conferences, some of them at the White House. He was an ardent advocate of Allied cooperation and selfless teamwork. He favorably impressed both the President and the Prime Minister. The British officers liked him. General Marshall watched with approval, laying his own plans for Eisenhower's future.

In the mid-February reorganization of the War Department, Eisenhower was appointed Marshall's Assistant Chief of Staff, in charge of War Plans. He and others of like mind, including General Carl Spaatz of the Army Air Corps, agreed that, with air supremacy, the invasion of Europe across the English Channel was feasible. Eisenhower worked out a cross-channel project which he submitted to the searching analysis of Marshall. In rough outline it was the same plan— even to a landing in Normandy rather than the Pas de Calais —which, with the help of many other minds, was so effectively followed on D-Day, two years and three months later.

The plan was approved by the President. It was also approved in principle by the British, but they found many practical difficulties in the way. Difficulties there were, indeed, but Moscow's clamor for a "second front" and the demand of the American public opinion for action as soon as possible, either in Europe or the Pacific, called both for a step-up in the production of war material and for someone who could bring American and British strategic concepts into closer alignment. Late in May 1942 Eisenhower, with the temporary rank of major general, was sent to London to start the job.

He spent ten days in England. His character, common sense, articulateness, and obvious devotion to duty made an excellent impression on the British allies. The visit forecast the tremendous success he was later to have in a role which demanded not only the qualities of a great soldier but also those of a diplomat and a statesman.

On Eisenhower's return to Washington it was decided that the time had come to establish a European Theater of Operations and to name its commander. Marshall asked Eisenhower for suggestions as to who should command. Eisenhower suggested Major General Joseph T. McNarney of the Army Air Corps. This is a sidelight on Eisenhower's "air mindedness"; he knew that McNarney believed the air forces could make possible the invasion of Europe by ground forces. The nomination was rejected. Marshall needed the capable McNarney on the General Staff.

Eisenhower then proceeded to draw up a directive for the future E.T.O. commander, whoever that might be. When he completed the directive he laid it on the Chief of Staff's desk, remarking that Marshall should read it in detail because of its importance to the prosecution of the war. Eisenhower relates that Marshall replied that he certainly did want to read it because "You may be the man who executes it." He added, "When can you leave?" It may be imagined that Eisenhower blurted, "Who, me?"

He was astonished. When he came to Washington less than six months before, he had secretly hoped at some time to command a division but had decided that, staff work considered, his chances were slender. He had never dreamed of high command in Europe. Three days after this conversation Marshall told him definitely that he was to head E.T.O. Eisenhower asked to have as an assistant Major General Mark Clark, whose work in the California maneuvers had won his respect. On June 23 he left by plane for England to take up his immense and epoch-making task. There he was soon to prove that Marshall's faith in him was amply justified.

The story of Allied trials and triumphs, of the cementing of the Anglo-American partnership, of the prodigious labors and mighty struggles which, under Eisenhower's direction, led at last to the complete destruction of the Nazi power, is now history. It has been well told by the General himself. It is necessary here only to touch on a few of the highlights of the man's record as he progressed from semi-obscurity to military fame and then to a world figure of almost unprecedented popularity. His progress was due as much to his innate Kansas simplicity as to his remarkable abilities.

At the time Eisenhower set up headquarters in London, continued Allied reverses left little reason for easy optimism about the road ahead. The Germans had won great victories in southern Russia, were pressing on toward the oil fields of the Caucasus. In Africa, Tobruk had fallen and Egypt was in danger. An understandable air of gloom greeted the new architect of unity. Eisenhower set about his administrative tasks with the aim of achieving an informal efficiency in the American headquarters and the greatest possible degree of cooperation with the British.

For a variety of reasons it had become apparent to Roosevelt and Churchill and to their military leaders that a major Allied operation was needed in 1942. It was equally evident that the cross-channel invasion would not be possible before 1943. The question was: Where could the Allies strike effectively with the means at hand? The answer was finally agreed upon in July. It was the invasion of North Africa. Mr. Churchill, who had been watching Eisenhower and had reached conclusions about him similar to those of Marshall six months earlier, agreed that the American general should command the joint venture.

The project opened a new chapter in the Eisenhower record, bringing to it drama and action. It called for months of careful planning, military and political. The French were the great uncertainty. Aside from de Gaulle's temperament, which had already caused trouble, the French of North Africa would not rally to him, and the British action against their fleet in 1940 still rankled. Yet they must be won over and added to the coalition. Secret negotiations with Allied sympathizers, which eventually called for General Clark's trip by submarine to the coast of Algeria, were begun. Plans were laid to smuggle the popular General Henri Giraud out of

Axis territory and make him the leader of the French effort.

On the eve of the landings General Eisenhower flew secretly to Gibraltar to direct operations. There, in one of his few quiet moments, the man from Kansas scribbled a philosophic memorandum which throws a revealing sidelight on his reaction to the high honors that had been thrust upon him. It is quoted by his naval aide, Lieutenant Harry Butcher:

"War brings about strange, sometimes ridiculous situations. In my service I've often thought or dreamed of commands of various types that I might one day hold—war commands, peace commands, battle commands, administrative commands, etc. One I now have could never, under any conditions, have entered my mind even fleetingly. *I have operational command of Gibraltar!!* The symbol of the solidity of the British Empire—the hallmark of safety and security at home—the jealously guarded rock that had played a tremendous part in the trade development of the English race! An American is in charge and I am he. Hundreds of feet within the bowels of the Rock itself I have my CP. I simply *must* have a grandchild or I'll never have the fun of telling this when I'm fishing, gray-headed on the banks of a quiet bayou in the deep south."

Troubles soon beset him. Giraud proved difficult; at first he demanded command of the whole operation. Giraud was not interested in politics—and the situation demanded skillful political handling. The French resistance ended in forty-eight hours and Eisenhower was faced with two problems. One was the military problem of bringing his scattered forces to bear quickly on the Axis fortress in Tunisia, 1,000 miles east of the westernmost Moroccan landings. The other was the political problem of uniting French North African army leadership against the Nazis.

Eisenhower proved himself essentially practical on both counts. He tried to get sufficient strength forward at once to take Tunis. But the rains came and his hopes were thwarted. He resigned himself to the necessity of building up the forces for a spring offensive.

Politically, he had to deal with realities. He had found in Algiers that the French Admiral Darlan, who had been one of the chief Vichy collaborationists and hated the British, was willing to change sides. Moreover, he seemed to be the one figure who at the moment could achieve French unity. Eisenhower decided to accept Darlan as the French leader, but to watch him carefully.

The decision aroused a storm of protest in Britain and the United States, especially among "liberal" elements who wanted nothing to do with ex-friends of the Nazis under any conditions. Eisenhower was put in the position of having to fight two wars simultaneously—the military and the political. But Darlan's assassination tended to quiet the uproar, and the eventual outcome of the North African project served to point up the wisdom of the commander's action.

Eisenhower's pragmatic approach to unexpected situations was again illustrated by the famous Patton episode during the conquest of Sicily. As we have seen, George Patton and Dwight Eisenhower had been friends for many years. Ike knew Georgie's strangely contradictory character, flamboyant, outwardly tough, inwardly sentimental. He recognized both Patton's limitations and his unique qualities as a hard-driving commander who got results.

When Patton, strained by his exertions in Sicily, lost his head and slapped a soldier whom he suspected of malingering in a hospital, Eisenhower recognized the grave effects of this action on public opinion in democratic America. It was enough to end a military career—and he badly needed Patton in the battles ahead. He came up with a practical solution. He did not shrink from disciplining his friend; he ordered him to make a public apology to the soldier. At the same time he wanted to play down the incident, to put it in perspective. He did not exercise censorship of the press; he merely presented the problem to the correspondents and asked their cooperation. They withheld the story. Eventually it came out. Patton's later record appears fully to have justified Eisenhower's attitude.

Italy surrendered. The long campaign up the Italian peninsula against the Germans began. Men and supplies from America were flooding across the Atlantic. As 1943 neared its end, the preparations for the crucial cross-channel invasion were speeded. On Christmas Eve, 1943, came the announcement that Eisenhower, who was now a full general, had been named Supreme Allied Commander in the West. In secrecy he made a brief trip home and returned to London in January. Then came nearly five months of stupendous Anglo-American effort to mount the invasion that was to end the war in Europe.

By this time Eisenhower's photogenic grin and his personal characteristics as reported by the press were familiar to the Allied world. But one factor of communication with the public was still lacking. He had established understanding with his troops, British and American, by the technique of chats with individuals on inspection tours and by the effective use of anecdotes in talks to units.

One story he used was about the British soldier who was seen blowing up his Mae West life jacket. Asked why, he replied: "This is the only bloody air support I'll get this day." From this, Eisenhower would lead to the moral of the story, "You men are going to have plenty of air support." Another concerned the two American soldiers who saw a four-star general ride by in his car. "That's a job I'd like," said one. Said the other: "Not for me; there's no chance of promotion." This always drew a laugh, which paved the way for the message Ike wanted to convey to his troops.

But the day came when he was to speak to a larger audience, though the message was directed to his soldiers.

D-Day in Normandy brought Eisenhower face to face with a momentous decision. The plans had been carefully drawn on the basis of tides and weather for the attack that could decide the fate of the United Nations. If not carried out during a short interval early in June the invasion must be postponed for two weeks, with added jeopardy to its success. The vast machine had been set in motion. Unexpectedly, the weather turned bad.

Eisenhower—who had thoughtfully prepared a statement assuming full responsibility for the failure of the invasion, if it were thrown back—ordered a twenty-four-hour postponement and took solitary counsel with himself. What he went through and how he assumed the responsibility was indicated by his reply to a question at a press conference after the war.

"In a decision like that, of course, there is one thing a commander faces," said Ike. "Sooner or later you have got to make it and you know it. You have got to say yes or no. That does something, I think, to prepare your mind for the thing. Decisions sometimes are suddenly presented and there has not been time for all the cold-blooded analysis, or to go around and see your subordinates and chat it over with them—that is sometimes a little soul-shaking." Soul-shaking though it was, Ike made the decision—on his own.

There followed weeks of agony and sublime courage on the beachhead, the breakthrough, the liberation of France, the last German counterthrust in the Battle of the Bulge, and the final sweep through the disintegrating Reich that Hitler had predicted would last for a thousand years. The Americans met the Russians along the Elbe. Hitler, Goebbels and Himmler died by their own hands. The Germans surrendered unconditionally to the Allied High Commander in a schoolhouse in Reims—and again, at Russian insistence, in Berlin.

Victory brought to General Eisenhower the plaudits of the Allied nations and the highest honors they could give. Among the honors was the Order of Victory of the Soviet Union which, conferred for the first time on a foreigner, was bestowed on Eisenhower by Russia's foremost soldier, Marshal Gregory Zhukov.

It is interesting to note Eisenhower's reaction to Russia at the moment of joint victory. The West then hoped for a One-World future, at the least for a live-and-let-live arrangement between Communist Russia and the rest of humanity. Eisenhower tried to foster cooperation, but there is conclusive evidence in *The Forrestal Diaries* (to be cited later) that he had a realistic distrust of Russian intentions, especially in Asia. In response to Soviet honors he rendered tribute to the Red Army. At the same time he made a plea for understanding which anticipated the later Russian propaganda "peace offensive." He said, in part:

"All of us who are right-thinking want the common men of all nations to have opportunities that we fought to preserve for them. They want the opportunities that will let all nations that have been engaged in this war go forward together to greater prosperity—not for us sitting around this table—but for the masses that we represent.

"That means peace. Speaking for the Allied forces, I say we are going to have peace even if we have to fight for it.

"On two occasions now I have had the great honor of meeting high officials of the Soviet Government. It is my feeling that in the basic desires of all of us they are one with us. Regardless of the methods by which we arrive at that goal, that is what we are struggling for.

"I cannot speak for any other individual. In fact, while I am expressing what is in my heart and mind, I am speaking for no one except Ike Eisenhower. But I believe that there is not any single man around this table that would not give back all the honors, all the publicity, everything else this war has brought to him, if he could have avoided the misery, the suffering, and the debt that have been brought to the populations by reason of this war.

"Yet this was a holy war. More than any other war in history, this war has been an array of the forces of evil against those of righteousness. It had to have its leaders and it had to be won—but no matter what the sacrifice, no matter what the suffering of populations, no matter what the cost, the war had to be won.

"To no one man do the United Nations owe a greater debt than to Marshal Zhukov. As our honored guest today he has come down and very courteously conferred certain honors of the Soviet Union upon members of the Allied forces. But Marshal Zhukov, being a modest man, probably underrates the standing that he holds in our hearts and minds.

"One day, when all of us here at this board are gathered to our fathers, there is certain to be another order of the Soviet Union. It will be the Order of Zhukov, and that order will be prized by every man who admires courage, vision, foresight and determination in a soldier.

"Gentlemen, I deem it a very great honor to ask you to rise and drink to Marshal Zhukov."

But the full measure of Eisenhower's ability to communicate his deepest feelings to the British and American publics was not seen until he was welcomed back to London on June

12, 1945, and given the rare honor of London citizenship in a stately ceremony at the Guildhall. There Ike Eisenhower of the Kansas prairies spoke his fundamental beliefs about democratic freedoms. It was an astonishingly effective oration, all the more so because the public was unaccustomed to such self-expression by military men. Winston Churchill, a rare judge of oratory, heartily congratulated the speaker. These are excerpts from the Guildhall address:

"The high sense of distinction I feel in receiving this great honor from the City of London is inescapably mingled with feelings of profound sadness. All of us must always regret that your great country and mine were ever faced with the tragic situation that compelled the appointment of an Allied Commander in Chief, the capacity in which I have just been so extravagantly commended.

"Humility must always be the portion of any man who receives acclaim earned in the blood of his followers and the sacrifices of his friends. Conceivably a commander may have been professionally superior. He may have given everything of his heart and mind to meet the spiritual and physical needs of his comrades. He may have written a chapter that will glow forever in the pages of military history. Still, even such a man—if he existed—would sadly face the facts that his honors cannot hide in the memories the crosses marking the resting places of the dead. They cannot soothe the anguish of the widow or the orphan whose husband or father will not return.

"The only attitude in which a commander may with satisfaction receive the tributes of his friends is in humble acknowledgment that no matter how unworthy he may be his position is a symbol of great human forces that have labored arduously and successfully for a righteous cause. Unless he feels this symbolism and this rightness in what he has tried to do, then he is disregardful of the courage, fortitude and devotion of the vast multitudes he has been honored to command. If all Allied men and women that have served with me in this war can only know that it is they whom this august body is really honoring today, indeed I will be content.

"This feeling of humility cannot erase, of course, my great

pride in being tendered the freedom of London. I am not a native of this land. I come from the very heart of America. In the superficial aspects by which we ordinarily recognize family relationships, the town where I was born and the one where I was reared are far separated from this great city. Abilene, Kansas, and Denison, Texas, would together add in size to possibly one five hundredth part of great London. By your standards those towns are young, without your aged traditions that carry the roots of London back into the uncertainties of unrecorded history. To those people I am proud to belong.

"But I find myself today five thousand miles from that countryside, the honored guest of a city whose name stands for grandeur and size throughout the world. Hardly would it seem possible for the London Council to have gone farther afield to find a man to honor with its priceless gift of token citizenship.

"Yet kinship among nations is not determined in such measurements as proximity of size and age. Rather we should turn to those inner things—call them what you will—I mean those intangibles that are the real treasures free men possess.

"To preserve his freedom of worship, his equality before the law, his liberty to speak and act as he sees fit, subject only to the provision that he trespass not upon similar rights of others a Londoner will fight. So will the citizen of Abilene.

"When we consider these things, then the valley of the Thames draws closer to the farms of Kansas and the plains of Texas. To my mind it is clear that when two peoples will face the tragedies of war to defend the same spiritual values, the same treasured rights, then in deepest sense those two are truly related. So even as I proclaim my undying Americanism, I am bold enough and exceedingly proud to claim the basis of kinship to you of London. And what man who has followed the history of this war could fail to experience inspiration from the example of this city?

"When the British Empire stood—alone but unconquered, almost naked but unafraid—to defy the Hitler hordes, it was on this devoted city that the first terroristic blows were launched. Five years and eight months of war, much of it on the actual battleline, blitzes big and little, flying V-bombs—

all of them you took in your stride. You worked, and from
your needed efforts you would not be deterred. You carried
on, and from your midst arose no cry for mercy, no wail of
defeat. The Battle of Britain will take its place as another of
your deathless traditions. And your faith and endurance have
finally been rewarded.

. . . .

"In London, my associates and I planned two great expeditions—that to invade the Mediterranean and later that to cross
the Channel. London's hospitality to the Americans, her
good-humored acceptance of the added inconveniences we
brought, her example of fortitude and quiet confidence in the
final outcome—all these helped to make the supreme headquarters of the two Allied expeditions the smoothworking
organizations they became.

"They were composed of the representatives of two proud
and independent peoples, both noted for its initiative and for
its satisfaction with its own customs, manners and methods.
Many feared that these representatives could never combine
together in efficient fashion to solve the complex problems
presented by modern war.

"I hope you believe we proved the doubters wrong. And,
moreover, I hold that we proved this point not only for war—
we proved it can always be done by our two peoples, provided only that both show the same good-will, the same forbearance, the same objective attitude that British and Americans so amply demonstrated in nearly three years of bitter
campaigning.

"No one man could alone have brought about this result.
Had I possessed the military skill of a Marlborough, the wisdom of Solomon, the understanding of Lincoln, I still would
have been helpless without the loyalty, vision, the generosity
of thousands upon thousands of British and Americans.

"Some of them were my companions in the High Command. Many were enlisted men and junior officers carrying
the fierce brunt of the battle. Many others were back in the
United States and here in Great Britain in London.

"Moreover, back of us were always our great national war
leaders and their civil and military staffs that supported and

31

encouraged us through every trial, every test. The whole was one great team. I know that on this special occasion the 3,000,000 American men and women serving in the Allied Expeditionary Force would want me to pay the tribute of admiration, respect and affection to their British comrades of this war.

"My most cherished hope is that, after Japan joins the Nazis in utter defeat, neither my country nor yours need ever again summon its sons and daughters from their peaceful pursuits to face the tragedies of battle. But—a fact important for both of us to remember—neither London nor Abilene, sisters under the skin, will sell her birthright for physical safety, her liberty for mere existence.

"No petty differences in the world of trade, traditions or national pride should ever blind us to identities in priceless values. If we keep our eyes on this guidepost then no difficulties along our path of mutual co-operation can ever be insurmountable. Moreover, when this truth has permeated to the remotest hamlet and heart of all peoples, then, indeed, may we beat our swords into plowshares and all nations can enjoy the fruitfulness of the earth."

In three and a half years the competent but unknown soldier had become the world figure who, on his return home soon afterward, was to have for the American people "such glamour as can wear sheer triumph out" and was given such adulation as few Americans have ever received. It was to his credit that he took it sensibly, modestly, with due enjoyment, but kept always his sense of perspective and felt himself to be merely an American who had been given an opportunity and had succeeded in a challenging job. It was Ike Eisenhower's faith that others could do likewise.

CHAPTER IV

Fame and Duty

It was natural that on his return home General Ike Eisenhower, the Supreme Commander of the great Allied armies, the victor of Europe—and the human being whose genial grin was known to millions—should have had a tumultuous welcome. He was given a triumph in Washington, where he addressed an enthusiastic joint session of Senators and Congressmen. In New York he rode for miles between lines of cheering people ("New York can't do this to a Kansas boy and keep its reputation for sophistication"), standing all a-grin in an open car with arms up-flung in a Churchillian V-for-victory symbol—or perhaps in a remembered West Point cheerleader's gesture. In Abilene he was welcomed with a parade of floats and with cherished home-town praise. America loved Ike and showed it.

It was also natural that there should be talk of Ike Eisenhower for President. The people of the United States have often sought to reward their military heroes with the highest office—and incidentally burden them with the greatest responsibility—in the land. A number of times they have succeeded, witness George Washington, Andrew Jackson, William Henry Harrison, Zachary Taylor, Ulysses S. Grant and Theodore Roosevelt. At other times they, or the party leaders who pick likely candidates, have failed.

The talk of Eisenhower for President started even during the war. It recurred during his triumphal tour, when he turned it off as a joke. Even at this early stage it became, however, so insistent that he had to take a stand. To one pressing inquiry by a reporter he replied: "In the strongest language you can command, you may say that I have no political ambitions at all. Make it even stronger than that if you can. I'd like to go further than Sherman in expressing myself on that

33

subject." (In 1884 General William Tecumseh Sherman, when offered the Republican nomination, said, "If nominated, I will not accept. If elected, I will not serve.")

This by no means prevented many Americans from believing that Ike Eisenhower had the qualities and the political appeal that fitted him for the presidency. Soon afterward, at the Potsdam Conference in July–August, 1945, Eisenhower was astounded when the subject was brought up in the course of a casual conversation by President Truman himself.

The conversation, as the General reported it in his *Crusade in Europe*, was to this effect: President Truman said, "General, there is nothing that you may want that I won't try to help you get. That definitely and specifically includes the presidency in 1948." In his surprise, Eisenhower treated the matter jocularly. With a laugh he replied, "Mr. President, I don't know who will be your opponent for the presidency, but it will not be I." In his account of the incident he added, "There was no doubt about *my* seriousness."

There was, indeed, no doubt of his seriousness. But the demand grew as the time approached to consider the presidential timber for 1948. In an interview in Miami in January, 1947, when he was Chief of Staff of the Army, Ike further defined his position in these words:

"From the beginning of the war whenever there was mentioned the possibility of a future political career for me I have instantly refused to consider such a contingency.

"It is clear that any mention of my name with politics is not good for the great organization I command. I am a soldier, and it is my duty to command the Army. The Army is definitely non-partisan and national in character and anything that tends to cloud the soundness of that feature is inimicable to the welfare of the United States."

The General's refusal to be considered as a candidate seems to have been based in part on his own modest estimates of his qualifications for political office and, perhaps in even larger part, on his understanding of the distrust which many Americans have for the idea of putting a military man in the supreme position of power in a nonmilitary democracy. Eisenhower's own beliefs, as indicated above, inclined him to agree, as a general proposition, with this distrust.

The matter is one that has to do with the so-called military mind. It has been argued that there is no such thing as the military mind; that the military men who have been presidents of the United States have succeeded or failed on their own qualities as leaders, not on the qualities that stemmed from their military life. The argument would seem to hold true in regard to some of the earlier military leaders who became presidents, for in general they were not military specialists, they were natural leaders who through force of circumstances became commanders in time of war of a democratic and often very undisciplined militia.

Yet in later years there came into being a military cast of mind which was a product of the specialized training given to the commanders of the nation's armed forces. It is an extremely well-trained mind in its specialized field, but a mind disciplined to obedience and order, inclined to be rigid and somewhat narrow. It is fitted to its own job, but there is a question as to how capable it is of coping with the fluid and often irrational complexities of high political office.

As we look at the record, these limitations seem to have had little bearing on the political qualifications of General Ike Eisenhower. Not only had he proved himself a great strategist; he had also shown in his welding together of the different national forces under his command a gift for diplomacy, and in the process he had proved himself to be a political leader of a very high order. Yet he modestly insisted on considering himself as merely a military leader.

Nevertheless, the Eisenhower-for-President boom continued. Polls of public opinion showed in 1947 that he could have easily won the nomination by either party. It was an almost unique situation in the history of the United States, where a political unknown, who had at that time given very little indication of what he thought about American political, economic or social problems, stood in high favor to lead the nation even though the people knew little of what he stood for. Already, Americans had sensed the need for the kind of leadership Eisenhower could provide, and his own selfless lack of political ambition merely fortified their trust in him.

Eventually he was forced to act. His action seems to have been based on two things: his own feeling that the misunderstanding of his position on the part of ardent supporters required a more definite statement, and his own disinclination to enter the political arena.

Finally, on January 22, 1948, he made his position unequivocally clear in the following letter to one of the leaders of the popular draft-Eisenhower movement, Leonard V. Finder, publisher of the Manchester, New Hampshire, *Evening Leader*. In it he disclosed his high sense of duty—and his belief that the time had not yet come for him to respond to the people's call to the highest of all duties.

"22 January, 1948

"Dear Mr. Finder:

"Your letter and editorial have been on my desk for more than a week while I pondered the reply merited by your obvious concern for the nation's welfare, and from a personal standpoint, by the honor you had done me. Months ago I thought that unqualified denial of political ambition would eliminate me from consideration in the coming campaign for the Presidency, because that office has, since the days of Washington, historically and properly fallen only to aspirants.

"That some few would misinterpret or look for hidden meanings in my past expressions was expected and discounted, but my failure to convince thoughtful and earnest men, such as yourself, proves that I must make some amplification. This will necessarily partake of the laborious, due to the complexity of the factors that have influenced me to say no more than I have, but which dictate my decision that I am not available for and could not accept nomination to high political office.

"I have heretofore refrained from making the bald statement that I would not accept nomination, although this has been my intention since the subject was first mentioned to me.

"This omission seems to have been a mistake, since it has inadvertently misled sincere and disinterested Americans. But my reticence stemmed from cogent reasons. The first was that such an expression would smack of effrontery. I had and

36

I have no desire to appear either as assuming that significant numbers of our people would actively interest themselves in me as a possible candidate, or to appear as lacking in respect and regard for the highest honor American citizens can confer upon one of their own body.

"A second and even deeper reason was a persistent doubt that I could phrase a flat refusal without appearing to violate that concept of duty to country which calls upon every good citizen to place no limitations upon his readiness to serve in any designated capacity. On this point it is my conviction that, unless an individual feels some inner compulsion and special qualifications to enter the political arena, which I do not, a refusal to do so involves no violation of the highest standards of devotion to duty.

"It was only the possible misinterpretation of my attitude that caused me concern and so long as I could believe that mere denial of political ambition would prevent serious misunderstanding and misdirected effort, I was reluctant to say more. It would seem almost superfluous for me to add that as long as I live I shall hold myself in instant readiness to respond to any call by the Government to military duty.

"In full awareness, then, and not in violation of my own sense of duty, I have developed the following conclusions, which are responsible for my negative decision.

"It is my conviction that the necessary and wise subordination of the military to civil power will be best sustained and our people will have greater confidence that it is so sustained when lifelong professional soldiers, in the absence of some obvious and overriding reasons, abstain from seeking high political office. This truth has a possible inverse application. I would regard it as unalloyed tragedy for our country if ever should come the day when military commanders might be selected with an eye to their future potentialities in the political field rather than exclusively upon judgment as to their military abilities.

"Politics is a profession: a serious, complicated and, in its true sense, a noble one.

"In the American scene I see no dearth of men fitted by training, talent and integrity for national leadership. On the other hand, nothing in the international or domestic situation especially qualifies for the most important office in the world a man whose adult years have been spent in the country's military forces. At least this is true in my case.

"I am deeply regretful if a too simple faith in the effectiveness of a plain denial has misled any considerable number concerning my intentions and so allowed them to spend time and effort under erroneous impressions. At the risk of appearing pompous, I must say that the honor paid me cannot fail to spur me, in future years, to work the more diligently for America, her youth, her veterans and all her citizens, and for the continuance of peace.

"I trust that this rather lengthy explanation will convince you that my conclusions are not only sound but have been arrived at objectively and have not been unduly influenced by my own desires and convenience. In any event, my decision to remove myself completely from the political scene is definite and positive. I know you will not object to my making this letter public to inform all interested persons that I could not accept nomination even under the remote circumstances that it were tendered me.

"With warm personal regards,

Sincerely,
Dwight D. Eisenhower"

Eisenhower's own conception of his place as a leader outweighed any feeling he may have had at the time of his duty to run for political office. As he then saw it, there were, at that time, no "overriding reasons" why he should accede to the popular demand of Eisenhower for President. What he wanted was to become the head of an educational institution where he thought he could carry on his service to the youth of America. The opportunity came with the call to become president of Columbia University.

PART II

The American Way of Life

"National solidarity is a requisite for national security."

CHAPTER V

Of Social Teamwork

"To define democracy in one word, we must use the word 'cooperation.'"

In order to see as clearly as possible what Dwight Eisenhower thinks about his country, its government, and its place in the world—to understand what his leadership means to the American people and how he is likely to stand on any given issue—it is necessary first to examine some of the basic concepts that he holds. These he has frequently set forth in his public utterances.

As has been said before, his position as a military man and his conscientious avoidance of political partisanship for that and other reasons have forced the statement of these concepts in broad terms. But that does not mean that they are meaningless generalities. From them, and from the background of his own life and actions, certain conclusions have been reached as to his social, political and economic thinking.

His social philosophy—the fundamental view he takes of humanity and its many problems—has, for example, been labeled "middle of the road." The term is a convenient one and sounds well, but it is not very exact. As a definition it lacks precision. How wide is the road? Who is the judge of its exact middle? The traveler himself may be certain that he is walking squarely down the middle, but to an observer on his right he may seem to be skirting the left-hand curb. Conversely, to a man watching from the left, he may seem well over on the right half of the highway.

To get at this question of what General Eisenhower's middle of the road attitude actually involves, a good starting point is the word "cooperation" in the above quotation. More than perhaps any other word in the language it typifies his instinctive approach to all questions of human relations—personal, political and economic, national and international. It was the guiding principle and the key to his success in the tremendously difficult task of welding diverse allies into a victorious combination in World War II. The word "cooperation" has been shown time and again to be one of the most fundamental tenets of his faith and thought.

Along with cooperation are certain principles which must be observed if there is to be real cooperation. These stem essentially from the Golden Rule. They were also laid down, as practical measures for political cooperation and for the insurance of the people's welfare, in the precepts and laws which the Founding Fathers established to guide the Republic. The principles and the working-together are inseparable.

This Eisenhower instinct for cooperation may derive in part from his inheritance from ancestors who profited by joint effort, in part from the family necessities of his boyhood, in part from the lesson of teamwork on the football field. It is allied to the General's practical view of matters; he doubtless sees most men as reasonable human beings who desire freedom, prosperity and peace, and who can attain all of them if they will work together for the common good. Cooperation among the people of the United States will preserve these benefits; cooperation among the peoples of the world will achieve them where they are lacking.

He is fortified in this belief by his reading of history. Our own country, in spite of a past filled with lively dissent, is a living monument to cooperation, from the first years when the settlers joined together to raise each other's cabins and to harvest each other's crops, to the present complex civilization which depends so heavily upon cooperation for its continued

40

functioning. Torn, as is inevitable, by rival interests of innumerable kinds, we must somehow compose our differences if we are to make the future we all have envisioned.

General Eisenhower sounded this note in one of his early talks soon after he returned from the war. In June, 1945, he told his fellow citizens of Abilene: "Through national organizations we cooperate with others in this world. It is through that conception that we hope to preserve the peace, and we cannot have any more wars. If we are going to cooperate effectively, we must first be united among ourselves."

Later, before the Economic Club of New York on November 20, 1946, he dwelt at greater length on the need for cooperation at all levels, from the individual to the governmental. He said:

"Woodrow Wilson said the highest form of efficiency is the spontaneous cooperation of a free people, and we proved that in war. We proved that this country, with free management, free labor, free enterprise, and free farmers, could utterly destroy a country like Germany that had regimented personnel in every activity. There is nothing that the United States cannot do if every man and woman in it—capitalist and laborer, Government and the people that are governed put their hearts into the accomplishment of the task.

"Every right-thinking American today is more concerned with the perpetuation of the fundamentals of the system that has made this country great than with any other single purpose. He must go back, if he is going to be useful in that crusade, and analyze what we have done in the past. He will find that it has been characterized by cooperation, and not by fighting among ourselves or refusing to see the other fellow's viewpoint. It has been a group effort, freely undertaken, that has produced the things of which we are so proud and which are represented in what we call the American way of life.

. . . .

"The cooperation that has made America great at home can be applied, if we work hard enough at it, to the whole world. If diverse creeds, races and group objectives can be sufficiently fused here at home so that we have become the

41

greatest and mightiest nation on the earth, similar cooperation and practical understanding can be extended throughout
the earth. There is room in the world for various systems of
government, provided only that there is mutual respect and
tolerance and provided always, and provided necessarily, that
no single one of these governments attempts to impose its
system on any other, no matter what the means used.

．　　　．　　　．　　　．　　　．　　　．　　　．

"Shortly after we had finished the Tunisian campaign and
a tremendous bag of Axis prisoners was in our hands, a group
of Allied officers visited my headquarters. They were getting
ready to set up in other areas of the world commands similar
to that then existing in the Mediterranean. They wanted the
secret of Allied success. They insisted upon charts; they
wanted to see where the black lines went and where the
dotted lines went. They wanted descriptions of the organizations. They wanted the charter by which we operated. It was
all very difficult because cooperative effort in war or peace is
based on mutual confidence and understanding and not upon
charts and charters. My answer to these people was: 'If you
sit down at the table with your opposite number and say:
"I've got something to do here and I wonder what that man
across the table is going to do to try to prevent me," you
won't get very far. But if you say to yourself: "That fellow
across the table is trying to win this war, and I wonder what
I can do to help," there will never be any difficulty in Allied
cooperation and your command has set up itself.'"

Eisenhower deeply feels that the fundamental principles
on which this country was founded and which guarantee the
individual liberties of its people formed the basis for the cooperation which made the country great. His middle-of-the-
road beliefs are directed toward the preservation of these
principles against dangers from within and from without.

His ideas in these regards were set forth in one of his best-
known speeches as the active president of Columbia University—that to members of the American Bar Association at
its annual meeting in St. Louis, on September 5, 1949. He
spoke to the lawyers in terms of the part they and their pro-

fession play in the American cooperative scheme of things, as he usually did to whatever group of the public he was addressing. These are two excerpts from that speech:

"Those who fear that our people are bogged down in the apathy of regimented thought, have never been privileged to listen in on the talk of a squad of soldiers or a gandy-dancer gang on the railroad. Or—for that matter—to a conference of bankers when there was under discussion a topic of vital interest to the future of this Republic. Readiness to air a grievance, to propose a remedy, to argue the pros and cons of a plan, is an enduring—and priceless—American trait.

"Few groups, however, can have so profound an impact on the course of public affairs as this assembly. Ours is a government of law—not of despotic decree—and you who practice the law have a specialized knowledge and unique influence in human relations. Indeed, without your counsel and advice hardly a single policy decision is reached by any of the forces most potent in the American economy—by labor organizations, by management, by farm groups, by welfare and professional associations, by government agencies. Your attitude today often foreshadows the facts of tomorrow.

"As a consequence, a more than ordinary responsibility is on you to remain free from bias and prejudice when you consider broad social problems. If you are true to your profession and to the responsibilities of your citizenship, you view them within a framework of *three fundamental principles* of American life.

"*First*, that individual freedom is our most precious possession. It is to be guarded as the chief heritage of our people, the well-spring of our spiritual and material greatness, and the central target of all enemies—internal and external—who seek to weaken and destroy the American Republic.

"*Second*, that all our freedoms—personal, economic, social, political—freedom to buy, to work, to hire, to bargain, to save, to vote, to worship, to gather in a convention or join in mutual association; all these freedoms are a single bundle. Each is an indispensable part of a single whole. Destruction of any inevitably leads to the destruction of all.

43

"*Third,* that freedom to compete vigorously among ourselves, accompanied by a readiness to cooperate wholeheartedly for the performance of community and national
functions, together make our system the most productive
on earth.

"These three principles express the common faith of loyal
Americans—the shining guide that, for the vast majority,
points always the straight path to America's future.

.   .   .   .   .   .

"For us *today,* those principles still dictate progress down
the center, even though *there* the contest is hottest, the progress sometimes discouragingly slow. The frightened, the defeated, the coward and the knave run to the flanks, straggling
out of the battle under the cover of slogans, false formulas
and appeals to passion—a welcome sight to an alert enemy.
When the center weakens piece-meal, disintegration and
annihilation are only steps away, in a battle of arms or of
political philosophies. The clear-sighted and the courageous,
fortunately, keep fighting in the middle of the war. They are
determined that we shall not lose our freedoms, either to
the unbearable selfishness of vested interest, or through the
blindness of those who, protesting devotion to the public
welfare, falsely declare that only government can bring us
happiness, security and opportunity.

"The middle of the road is derided by all of the right and
the left. They deliberately misrepresent the central position
as a neutral, wishy-washy one. Yet here is the truly creative
area within which we may obtain agreement for constructive
social action compatible with basic American principles, and
with the just aspirations of every sincere American. It is the
area in which are rooted the hopes and allegiance of the vast
majority of our people."

Humanitarianism is one of the deep qualities of American
life, an essential part of the American creed. How the General feels on this subject, how he thinks of helping the unfor-
tunate as part of his concept of cooperation, was expressed in
an address to the meeting of the United Jewish Appeal in
Washington on February 23, 1947. There he voiced his con-

cern for the problems of minority groups, both in this country and abroad. He said:

"No matter how we may answer the question 'Am I my brother's keeper?' the implications of the question have such inescapable effects on the effort to produce world order that the example you provide may well bear fruit in the attack on world problems of unlimited scope. Possibly it may help us to realize that there can be no security for one unless it is enjoyed by all; that though force can protect in emergency, only justice, fairness, consideration and cooperation can finally lead men to the dawn of eternal peace. Certainly your example should help us see that enlightened self-interest demands the elimination of the unfair practices against large segments of mankind which, in the past, have so blackened the history of humanity.

"Humanitarianism is a link that binds together all Americans. As great as is our love of freedom, equally great is the American feeling of compassion for those in distress. Whenever tragedy or disaster has struck in any corner of the world, the American people has promptly and generously extended its hand of mercy and help. Generosity has never impoverished the giver; it has enriched the lives of those who have practiced it. In this postwar world, with its bewilderment and fear, Americans can still be thankful that we are in a position to give rather than dependent for our very existence upon the mercy of others. One of the privileges of this great democracy has been its opportunities for us to share with those less fortunate. And the bread we have cast upon the waters has been returned in blessings a hundredfold."

It is evident that the Eisenhower social creed includes the belief that the middle-of-the-road cooperative life imposes upon all Americans, from the big business magnate to the unskilled laborer, duties and obligations that must be met if that life is to continue.

Powerful business organizations engaged in the marketing and advertising of the products of American industry have an especial opportunity and an especial duty to promulgate the intrinsic values of the American way of life. Reading between the lines, one may conclude that, by the same token,

Eisenhower feels that these organizations should so govern themselves as to serve the concept of cooperation rather than to use their vast power for selfish, immediate gain.

At a luncheon of the Sales Executives Club in New York on September 21, 1948, soon after he became president of Columbia University, he said:

"I am convinced that what we need today among us far more than a further education in the obscure, in the refined research, even in the fields of basic science and so on, is education in the obvious, and I believe in attempting to bring home such a lesson as that with respect to our future in this country. There is a service to be performed, because—and associating you instantly with the effort—I believe that when you sell an automobile, or a tire, or a refrigerator, or a service, or anything else, you are not merely selling that article, although it may be the best in the world. You are selling a product of America, and more than that, a part of America.

"I believe that salesmen who convey to the public the products of our system are in a peculiarly advantageous position to keep before us all the obvious things that we hold and must never forsake."

Eisenhower's admiration for the courage of the founders of the American system and his insistence that their spirit be passed on to the coming generations of Americans was voiced in an impromptu talk of American history to a high school class in Chicago in March, 1949:

"The wonderful courage and bravery of the colonists, setting out on a perilous trip to a new land, is something we have come to take too much for granted. It all happened so long ago—we forget what they did and why they did it. They did it because they were determined to live their lives the way they wanted to live. No one was going to tell them what they should think, what they should say, how they should worship, how they should work and play and live.

"You here, today—all of us—are the inheritors of their courage and the ideals they stood for. Today we can go to the schools we want to, attend the church we choose, we can do the job we want to do. We don't have to listen to anyone else.

46

"Our ancestors fought hard to establish this freedom for us, and in my opinion we have to fight hard to keep it. Because if it isn't worth fighting for it isn't worth keeping. When we no longer value these freedoms, then we are not going to have them. . . . We'll be living under the whip. We'll be told what we can do or cannot do, and what we shall think, instead of working and living the way we want to, in freedom, the way we do now.

"So no matter what the books say today, I believe that each one of us must remember when we read about the contribution the colonists made to American history and the American way of life that it took an awful lot of courage to start, and I urge all of you that you do not forget, above all things, that that courage is one of our rich inheritances, courage and the love of freedom."

These examples indicate the broad aspects of Eisenhower's social beliefs, of those ideals which he thinks should govern human relations, and, more specifically, the rules of conduct that are a pole star to the American people in this time of questioning and trial of our institutions.

His beliefs are simple and basic—in the freedom of the individual and in the individual's consequent obligation to be honest in his dealings with his fellow man, in the necessity for intelligent and unselfish cooperation to preserve freedom, in the virtues of private initiative and the reward of hard work, in the need for all members of society to accept the duties and obligations which they are called upon to bear as free Americans.

Cynics may consider these as generalizations which have little bearing on the business of getting one's share of things. They may, with reason, inquire how these ideals can be put to practical application in an uncertain world where human beings are all too obviously intent on grabbing power or trying to assure themselves of security.

But it should be remembered that "without faith the nations perish." Dwight Eisenhower's ideas about social behavior are, to him, both rules of conduct and articles of faith in the ability of mankind to progress toward better things. In their sum they constitute his notions of "Americanism."

CHAPTER VI

Of People and Government

"Our American heritage is threatened as much by our own indifference as it is by the most unscrupulous office-seeker or by the most powerful foreign threat. The future of this Republic is in the hands of the American voter."

General Eisenhower himself has made clear that his political thinking stems from and is part and parcel of the broad social attitudes which have just been examined. As duty and integrity are guiding principles in his own life, he believes that each citizen has his duty toward his country and its government—and that the government, in turn, owes the primary duty to its citizens of protecting their rights and securing for them the greatest degree of individual liberty commensurate with the welfare of the public—of the *whole* public.

There are two major facets to his political thinking as revealed in his own words. One concerns the freedoms and rights which were won by our English and American forefathers and the part government should play in protecting them. The other facet concerns the danger, at all times and in all countries but more especially in the turmoil of the present age, that the growing power of government will destroy its primary function by encroaching on the very rights and liberties it was established to insure.

Once, asked by a reporter from *Stars and Stripes* for his definition of the basis of American democracy, he replied:

"The faith of all our people in our way of living, the equality of all men before the law, the understanding that man is not just a superior animal, but a thinking individual, and the man-in-the-street's dislike for any form of authoritarianism."

On the second score—the danger from statism—Eisenhower feels strongly, as he has indicated on many occasions. The danger is both external and internal. Abroad it is represented at its worst by Communist dictatorship. At home its peril comes from the often well-meant extension of government services—and controls—over the lives of the individual citizens. Not that such extensions are not at times necessary to cope with the growing complexities of modern life and to defend the nation from its enemies. But any such extension must be examined with critical eyes to see whether it furthers or endangers the basic purposes of the American form of government. To judge this matter is the great responsibility of the American citizen.

In an address on September 24, 1947, at the University of West Virginia, where he was presented with an honorary degree, Eisenhower said:

"Human dignity, economic freedom, individual responsibility, these are the characteristics that distinguish democracy from all other forms devised by man. This democratic system, this capitalistic system, has given to our people the highest standard of living this world has ever known and has made of this nation a force for justice and peace.

"If any say, as has been said, that they cannot live side by side in this world with democracy, then the conclusion must be based upon their own conviction of the inferiority of their own system. Democracy's goal in the world, as it is at home, is peace, peace based on justice, on right, on human understanding, on cooperation.

"Should we ever permit aggression from without to reach us in overwhelming force, if we ourselves should tamper with its foundations, all this world would be lost. If we engage in the ill-conceived experiments of the past, or weaken then under transient pressure, we should jeopardize the one way of life that has proved able to provide the maximum of human liberty with the maximum of common good."

His thoughts on American democracy were expanded later in a talk he gave on June 26, 1948, at the dedication of an addition to the plant of the International Business Machines Corporation at Poughkeepsie, New York. He said:

"The political freedoms we know, the American concept of democracy, certainly include a faith, related to some religion, that man is more than an animal, that he possesses a soul.

"If we have not that faith, then why should any of us admit that any other is born with equal rights to himself? Each of us instinctively recognizes, and our forefathers so stated, that an individual, because he was born, possesses certain rights. And to prove that we must go back and depend upon faith, and faith alone; and I say it is a faith, akin to religion, to most of us.

"It depends upon a system of free enterprise because eventually if any government of any individual—or in any other way all property residing within a nation's borders were owned by the government or by a particular small group of individuals, there would be no recourse for that government or for those individuals except to order each of us in the way of life we must follow, in order to make that tremendous, staggering business a success.

"Without free enterprise, the political freedom we know cannot exist, because if that government has to order each of us to do our job, it could not permit strikes, it could not permit incitement to strike, and freedom of the press, which is the very foundation upon which our whole system of political freedom depends, would disappear.

"Finally, there must be included in any concept of democracy, as we attempt to practice it, a readiness to cooperate in the performance of our functions—such functions as the national security and the establishment of rule and order among us so that even our own system, with all its virtues, may not fall prey to its own weaknesses, may not be exploited by people of evil intent."

The General's historical view of the development of democracy and the danger to it, now and in the future, from the encroachment of statism were outlined in his address to the Sales Executives Club, on September 21, 1948. The word statism seems to stand in his mind not only for foreign dictatorships, but for any highly centralized, overgrown system of government which takes upon itself the functions of local government to the detriment of the duties and initiative of the people. Our love of freedom and dislike of centralized control he sees as going back for centuries, to the Magna Carta and before. He said:

"The English-speaking race has certainly proved time and again, and more particularly since 1215 and Runnymede, that the one thing for which it will sacrifice everything, including its life, is its freedoms; so those freedoms become almost the very reason for which we exist to enjoy them and to pass them on unalloyed to our children and to our grandchildren.

"And, in connection with that thought, we frequently hear this expression: 'Some'—let me use the word—'mountebank is constantly saying to us, because we believe in a system of competitive or free enterprise as an essential of our system, that we are upholding property rights as against human rights.'

"I could believe that is an entirely false view. A property right is merely one of the human rights, and if it is not sustained, all the others will disappear!

"It seems to me that if we can conceive of a state where the title to all property, and to everything that is necessary for the sustenance of the human race, can pass into the hands of government, oligarchy, any kind of centralized organization, that eventually we must face the fact that that government must, of necessity, direct us by order as to what we shall do. There will be complete regimentation; in other words, dictatorship, and there is no escape from that concept."

A month later, in October, 1948, he again sounded this theme in his talk before the meeting of the Association of National Advertisers:

"The first thing, it seems to me, as we contemplate a picture of America, is what made it.

"It has not been merely limitless amounts of natural

51

wealth. It has not been the fact that these resources were virgin and untouched for us to seize and use. Instead, it has been an underlying spiritual unity born out of the belief that man is a dignified human being created in the image of his Maker and by that fact is the possessor of certain inalienable rights.

"We usually refer to this group of rights and privileges as our Bill of Rights—the first ten amendments to our Constitution. But, I think, that the first thing we should realize is that all of these rights are a bundle. They are like a vast building, each of them is an indispensable stone in the stability of the whole. Remove one, and all the others must, of necessity, fall.

"Now, the right that seems to have come under attack in our day and time more than any other is the right to property. Many people have tried to make us believe that there is an essential antagonism between so-called property rights and human rights.

"This, to my mind, is the fallacy which underlies the conflict now going on in the world between statism and the system of exercise of our freedoms.

"Statism comes before us in many different guises and with many different appeals. It points up—with great emphasis—any of the errors, the mistakes, in the application of the democratic principles. It points, for example, to the depression of the '30's, and to the eleven million in the breadlines. But it fails to state that under a statist form of government all of those people would probably be in salt mines working under the whip and the bayonet."

The inaugural address which it is the duty of every incoming college president to deliver on being invested with office, gives the new president an opportunity to express his stand on as many subjects as he feels proper. In that address, on October 12, 1948, which was devoted in part to his views on the function of education in a democracy, Eisenhower spoke of his philosophy of government and his dislike of centralization. His address contained this significant passage:

"The concentration of too much power in centralized government need not be the result of violent revolution or great

52

upheaval. A paternalistic government can gradually destroy, by suffocation in the immediate advantage of subsidy, the will of a people to maintain a high degree of individual responsibility. And the abdication of individual responsibility is inevitably followed by further concentration of power in the state. Government ownership or control of property is not to be decried principally because of the historic inefficiency of governmental management of productive enterprises; its real threat rests in the fact that, if carried to the logical extreme, the final concentration of ownership in the hands of government gives to it, in all practical effects, absolute power over our lives."

Our present democracy and the duties of its citizens are firmly rooted in the early history of our country and the political faiths which resulted in our Constitution. In his address at the 195th Commencement Exercises of Columbia University, June 1, 1949, General Eisenhower again stressed the debt we owe to the colonists who risked all to make the United States a free nation. He said:

"When Columbia's first graduating class was awarded its degrees, the pace and tempo of the human world had changed little from the days of the Caesars and the Pharaohs. Life then, as viewed from our observation post two hundred years later, had in it more of leisure and less of strain; more of meditation and less of hysteria; more of faith and confidence and less of doubt and fear. But underneath the surface, in the generation of Columbia's founders, there was spreading the spiritual fire of a new social and political philosophy, based upon the concept of equality of right among men, regardless of the accident of birth.

"For centuries that fire had glowed so feebly as frequently to disappear almost completely from view; but it persisted sufficiently to provide much of the inspiration for the great trans-Atlantic migration of the seventeenth and eighteenth centuries. Many diverse reasons hardened men and women of Europe to an ocean journey that was then scarcely less than terrifying. Foremost was a fervent hope that they would find in the New World escape from ancient tyrannies imbedded in the Old World's structure. This purpose expanded and flourished at amazing speed in the American wilderness, where only individual courage, self-confidence and faith could spell survival. It begot in our fathers a determination to reject utterly any political theory that gave one man, or a group of men, an inherent right to dominate others—a determination eloquently expressed and reaffirmed in our most treasured historical documents.

"In the simple living of that day the application of this resolve to social and political problems, while difficult, did not involve such complexities and confusions that our forefathers were led to deny the validity of their principles. But, since the days of Columbia's founders, a mighty upsurge in the gathering of knowledge and the development of machines has many times over complicated human relations. Technologically, we—who are gathered here—and our predecessors of Columbia's first Commencement are separated by the chasm between the ox-cart and the jet engine, between the grist mill and the cyclotron, between a man wresting his own living out of a wilderness farm and the citizen whose livelihood depends on the successful functioning of an entire and complex national economy.

.   .   .   .

"Infallible counsel for each of us is to be found within our valid hopes and aspirations and ideals as human beings, so clearly understood by our colonial forebears. The simple faith, the unshakable conviction they held in man's individual rights and his equality before the law and God, is the most priceless jewel in all the vast spiritual and material heritage those men and women bequeathed to us. We cannot afford to lose their sharp sense of basic values—expressed by Patrick Henry in one imperishable sentence."

The limitations on the place of government in democracy and the need for people to fulfill their obligations as free and equal citizens were dealt with concisely in a still later address. This was before the annual *Herald Tribune* Forum in New York on October 24, 1949. The title of the address was

"The Individual's Responsibility for Government." The pertinent excerpt follows:

" 'What Kind of Government Ahead? The Responsibility of Every Citizen.' *There*, in ten words, is the most important question of our day and the nub of the American political philosophy.

"We believe in human dignity, in human rights not subject to arbitrary forfeiture or curtailment. We believe that these rights can be fully possessed and effectively exercised only so long as man asserts and maintains himself the master, not the serf, of institutions he creates. Unless he is free to use his birthright, it is worthless—in fact, does *not* exist. Freedom, however, is not unbridled license. Nor is it merely the expression of the jungle instinct to survive and dominate.

"Free men, consequently, agree upon certain rules—which we call laws—and maintain political agents, or governments, to codify and enforce upon us all these self-imposed rules. In free countries, the agent may never become the master; if human rights and freedoms are to flourish, government must operate with its powers sharply defined and limited *by* the governed.

"And unless we understand this, the American Dream may become the American Nightmare.

"For us Americans, the original limits on the authority conceded to the federal government are the Constitution and the Bill of Rights. But, the dividing line between government's functions, on the one hand, and the individual's rights, privileges and inescapable responsibilities never is completely fixed; never is static. It oscillates constantly, in a middle area between centralized authority and individual liberty, as economic, social and political conditions require more, or less, action by government. War certainly demands a mass control intolerable in peace. Even peacetime crises may argue for a *temporary* surrender of some personal liberties for the alleged good of the public."

From these evidences it seems certain that General Eisenhower considers himself middle of the road, politically as well as in his broad social concepts. But here again we come to the difficulty of defining the term. For all his admiration for pioneer virtues, it is clear from many other evidences that Eisenhower would not wish to put back the clock, to undo certain social and political measures that have wrought changes in American life since 1930. Some of them he must unquestionably regard as needed improvements. Others he seems to regard as dangers.

He apparently believes that a number of the reforms of the past two decades have achieved their purpose in bettering life for the majority of Americans, but that extension of the principles they established may result in the further spreading of governmental power into fields alien to it before 1930. Compromise and cooperation will keep the benefits and avert the dangers. Individual responsibility and morality must have greater play.

Thus, when viewed from the standpoint of the Roosevelt New Deal and its aftermath, Eisenhower appears to be walking on the right, or conservative, side of the middle way. But looked at from the viewpoint of the more conservative elements of the Republican party his idea of progress is probably seen in different terms.

CHAPTER VII

Of American Economics

"I believe that without free enterprise
there can be no democracy."

The economic thinking of General Eisenhower centers,
like his social and political thinking, around the word "cooperation." In his view, the nation has become great because it was founded on the concept of individual freedom,
because it has been a land of opportunity for all, and because
its system of free enterprise—although competitive, and bene-
ficially so in the productive sense—is in the last analysis based
upon a partnership between all the major elements of the
producing population.

The success of both democracy and free enterprise depends upon the qualities of leadership and responsibility dis-
played by the leaders of the various segments of the economic
body. This means not just a responsibility to further the interests of their particular groups, but a responsibility to aid
in the cooperative development of the economy as a whole
and for the benefit of all the people. This calls for partnership
between management and labor and capital to their mutual
advantage. It also requires an economic flexibility that is
capable of adjustment to changing conditions and that is able
over the years to utilize new production methods and skills
to aid the steady advance of the American living standard.

That the American system of free enterprise has this
flexibility seems to be one of Eisenhower's cardinal beliefs.
He points to the history of its development as proof. It has
had its ups and downs, its internal struggles and its injustices,
but it has done more, in the last century and a half, to improve the living standards and increase the material comforts
of the average man than any other system in the world.

That is why the Marxian doctrine of inevitable class struggle has no basis in fact and no application whatever to the American scene. It is founded upon a century-old concept of injustice to workers in the developing machine age which has been changed by social reform and increased efficiency, and upon European class distinctions which America happily escaped. Measured against the realities of the American economic system, it makes no sense. The enviable status of the American worker and of Americans in general is the proof definite.

This being so, defense of capitalism and the free enterprise system does not make one a "reactionary." On the other hand, the success of the system does not free one from the obligation to strive continually for further improvement. Using the freedom and initiative for personal betterment which the system provides, Americans must also keep always in mind their duties to each other.

Some of these beliefs were concisely stated in one paragraph of President Eisenhower's Commencement Address at Columbia on June 8, 1950. He said:

"Determination to support and sustain the political and economic freedom of the individual does not make us reactionaries, except in fuzzy minds or among those egoists who seek the right to dominate us—always, of course, for our own good. Americans have never been afraid to adjust procedures and methods to a changing economy. On the contrary, it has been clear from the beginning that our system fosters and requires adjustment to change; it demands growth that is rooted in the vitalizing, unending effort of free individuals to work out for the good of all the problems that confront them. Stagnation would be as disastrous to the Republic as would unwise innovations not rooted in the vital purposes of our national charter."

This country as a land of opportunity for the youth of today he brought out again in an address to the First Columbia College Forum on Democracy on February 12, 1949. Youth has its responsibilities for the future of the people as well as do other generations, and his concern that young people should know something of the origins of the freedoms we enjoy, appreciate their value and carry them on to the future appears in a number of his talks. On that occasion he said in part:

"And to come down specifically to today and to youth. I believe that opportunity is greater today—and I mean individual opportunity—than it has ever been at any time in our history because opportunity, regarded in the sense that Lincoln regarded it, is this: opportunity to serve the society to which you belong. And, frankly, when our democracy with its system of free enterprise is operating properly, then individual reward comes about in the measure that you render service to others.

"All about us with the changing economic scene, with concentrations of great labor groups in cities, with the dependence of the farm and city each upon the other and still unable to find ways in which they can get along together, problems of distribution, surpluses in one area and starvation in another, there are thousands of things to which you gentlemen can apply your talents and with great opportunity to do good for your great country and, by doing so, to receive greater rewards for yourself than has ever been the case in the past. And that, I honestly feel, gentlemen, includes even the days of the Revolution and of the War Between the States."

Eisenhower linked his belief in democracy and economic freedom with the moral and religious beliefs of the American people in an address when he received *The Churchman* Award for the Promotion of Good Will and Better Understanding Among All Peoples on December 3, 1946. He said:

". . . I am proud to say that I am a fanatical devotee of the American system of democracy. I believe that the two fundamentals of the American democracy are, first, a deep and abiding religious faith, and, second, a system of freedoms and rights for the individual that we generally refer to loosely and roughly as 'free enterprise.'

"With respect to the first, I can see no reason for the worship of the democratic principles that gives to all equal rights before the law, unless we recognize in each of us something other than a mere educated animal.

"If there is not a soul that is related in some way to a religious Being, no matter what the faith, then I can see no reason why each of us should not exploit to the full any talent he may have vis-à-vis his fellow, vis-à-vis his neighbor, and take advantage if he possibly can.

"Our system denies us the right to do that. We have equality before the law. And unless there is some conviction of the value of this thing that we call the soul, there is no excuse for democracy. Therefore, I say that, fundamentally, one of the foundation stones of democracy is a deep and abiding religious faith among the masses of people that practice democracy."

But the talk which is generally considered to embody most clearly and forcefully his ideas about the economics of our country is that he made at the American Bar Association meeting at St. Louis on September 5, 1949. Although he covered a variety of subjects, the major part of the address was devoted to economic matters. These are pertinent excerpts:

"In the industrialized economy of the twentieth century, that path lies down the middle of the road between the unfettered power of concentrated wealth on one flank, and the unbridled power of statism, or partisan interest, on the other. Our agreement in these three great fundamentals provides the setting within which can always be composed any acute difference.

"Yet there are some who build out of catch-words and fallacies a testament of inescapable conflict within our economy. Should misguided or vicious persons gull us into acceptance of this false dogma, the fault—criminal and stupid—will be our own. We will have been victimized by the crude technique of the brazen lie, often repeated. You, of the legal profession, are uniquely fitted to expose this fraud, and thereby prevent senseless cleavage and hostility among us.

. . . . . .

"Selfishness and cupidity . . . will never be wholly eradicated from within us. But just as we do not, today, seek to solve international problems in terms of war-time passion,

60

let us not confuse present industrial difficulties with the mistakes and failures of past decades, long since corrected. In the infancy of our modern industrialized society, management and labor and the neutral observer were often equally ignorant of sound practice, of economic trends, of the effect of mass production on human standards of living. However, guided by great principles and lighted by the spirit of fair play, the builders of our industrial economy have achieved success that confounds the prophets of disaster.

"A little more than a century ago the *Communist Manifesto* of Karl Marx was published, preaching the falsehood of an inescapable class warfare that would continue within such a society as ours until by violence the workers erased all traces of traditional government. If Marx were right, this day should be, in all our great country, an annually recurring provocation to riot, physical strife and civil disorder. The factual evidence of his blunder is so clear that it ought not to require emphasis.

"Nevertheless, with a full century of contrary proof in our possession and despite our demonstrated capacity for cooperative teamwork, some among us seem to accept the shibboleth of an unbridgeable gap between those who hire and those who are employed. We miserably fail to challenge the lie that what is good for management is necessarily bad for labor; that for one side to profit, the other must be depressed. Such distorted doctrine is false and foreign to the American scene where common ideals and purpose permit us a common approach toward the common good. It must be combated at every turn by both clear word and effective deed.

"Of course, our path in places is still obstructed by unfinished business and the debris of inequities and prejudices, not yet overcome. But, strong in the fundamental principles of American life, we have, in less than two centuries, accomplished more for the community of men than was won in the previous forty.

.   .   .   .   .   .

"Thus, the American system in line with its principles can and does, by governmental action, prevent or correct abuses springing from the unregulated practice of a private economy. In specific cases local governments have, with almost unanimous approval, provided needed public services so that extraordinary power over all citizens of the community might not fall into the hands of the few. In all cases we expect the government to be forehanded in establishing the rules that will preserve a practical equality in opportunity.

"We, in turn, carefully watch the government—especially the ever-expanding Federal government—to see that in performing the functions obviously falling within governmental responsibility, it does not interfere more than is necessary in our daily lives. We instinctively have greater faith in the counter-balancing effect of many social, philosophic, and economic forces than in arbitrary law. We will not accord to the central government unlimited authority, any more than we will bow our necks to the dictates of the uninhibited seekers after personal power in finance, labor, or any other field.

"Extremists hope that we lack the stubborn courage, the stamina and the intelligent faith required to sustain the progress of the attack. By appeals to immediate and specialized selfish advantage, they would blind us to the enduring truth that no part of our society may prosper permanently except as the whole of America shall prosper. They use the cloying effect of subsidy as well as the illusory promise of an unearned and indolent existence to win our acceptance of their direction over our lives. They believe that the intricate interdependencies of our highly industrialized economy will drive us to desert principles in favor of expediencies—particularly the expediency of governmental intervention.

"Thus far the record belies their hopes. Consider the abundance of courage and faith, manifested thousands of times each year in union meetings when working men penetrate the ideological complexities, parliamentary maneuvers, entangled plottings of Communist agitators, exposing and defeating them. Consider also the many thousands of times each year in meetings of management when businessmen—though primarily charged with concern for cost, production, distribution, and profit—subordinate those material things to increasing the welfare of their employees. Were it not for those, in both management and labor, who fight and work to keep us from the ditches on the right and left, then indeed this day [Labor Day] would be a symbol of class warfare, and . . . St. Louis—and every other great industrial city—would be a battle ground for what Marx called the proletariat.

"But, in public places, soon only the specious promises of the extreme right and the extreme left may make themselves heard. The truth can be lost if the peddlers of lies go unchallenged. To defeat them in their campaign of falsehood, we must first destroy their stock in trade—the shibboleth of an irreconcilable difference between those who manage and those who operate.

"Marx appealed to the self-pity, the justifiable resentments of the proletariat in the Europe of his day. He could not imagine a great nation in which *there is no proletariat,* in which labor is the middle class that he so much despised and hated. He could not foresee that millions of plain people would, in two World Wars, stake all they possessed in defense of ideas and ideals that were hardly more than shadowy dreams to most Europeans of a century ago. He could not imagine that one day the grave of an unidentified soldier would become a symbol of our dedication to political, economic and social freedom.

. . . .

"You realize that the interests of labor and management in most situations are identical. Differences are centered almost exclusively in the annual bargaining conferences. But even here the true differences are far more apparent than they are real. For intelligent management certainly recognizes the need for maximum income to workers, consistent with reasonable return on investment. With equal clarity, labor cannot fail to recognize the need for increasing amounts of risk capital to provide jobs for our constantly growing population. And—make no mistake about it—no group in our country is more firmly dedicated to the retention and development of our system of private competitive enterprise than is American Labor.

"The vast majority of Americans, moreover, respects your historic role in the development of the American way of life and your unique position in relation to its continued progress.

For one thing—if you set yourselves to the job—you can clean out the ambush of catchwords, tags and labels in which the plain citizen, including the old soldier, is trapped every time he considers today's problems. How can we appraise a proposal if the terms hurled at our ears can mean anything or nothing, and change their significance with the inflection of the voice? Welfare state, national socialism, radical, liberal, conservative, reactionary and a regiment of others—these terms in today's usage, are generally compounds of confusion and prejudice. If our attitudes are muddled, our language is often to blame. A good tonic for clearer thinking is a dose of precise, legal definition.

"Above all, we need more economic understanding and working arrangements that will bind labor and management, in every productive enterprise, into a far tighter voluntary cooperative unit than we now have. The purpose of this unity will be—without subordination of one group to the other—*the increased productivity that alone can better the position of labor, of management, of all America.* No arbitrary or imposed device will work. Bureaucratic plans, enforced on both parties by Government, pave the road to despotism. Laws that needlessly impose stifling controls and inflexible rules beyond the codes necessary to fair play may be necessary in a dictatorship—but in a democracy, they are futile at the best and the cause of rebellion at the worst.

"You, however, using your recognized position as guardians of the law and counsel to both parties in dispute, can work out voluntary solutions in our industrial relations—that now sometimes appear to be no better than a state of armed truce, punctuated by outbreaks of industrial warfare. Such a condition is a criminal absurdity, since the participants possess a common stake in the prosperity of industry. Moreover, they possess common political concepts, social purpose, economic attitude and, above all, identical aspirations for themselves, their families, their country.

"They are Americans—all."

In the second of his two major speeches on this subject, Eisenhower stressed the necessity for promoting social and economic welfare without jeopardy to freedoms and rights.

These beliefs, with that sense of historical perspective which he has so often shown, were embodied in his talk at the Eighteenth Annual New York *Herald Tribune* Forum on October 24, 1949, when he said:

"At home we face the complex social, economic and political problems that have been highly complicated for democracy by the industrial revolution. We have had to adjust precepts, doctrine, and methods developed in an agrarian frontier age to the industrialized economy and civilization of the twentieth century. This has not been easy. Perfection has *not* been attained, but we will continue to seek it, using every means available to us.

"A century ago, the year of the discovery of gold in California, the average American citizen typified a sturdy independence. He had faith and confidence in himself and in the limitless potential of his country's resources readily available to his use. While vaguely aware of his government's existence, it had little to do, either good or bad, with his day-by-day living. With a mite of help, the citizen built his own house from materials at hand. He raised his family's food—and good land was to be had cheaply. His clothing was made by his wife; his transport was his horse. Given health, initiative and stamina, he could always find himself and his dependents subsistence—even in abundance. Taxes were low, opportunity was everywhere, life was good—even if frequently filled with risk and danger to life and limb. In a sense, the aims of the framers of our Constitution seemed to be almost perfectly achieved.

"Nevertheless, the essential dignity of man and the mastery of man over his institutions were less expressed in the facts of American life in 1849 than they are in 1949. Then, luxuries were for the very few, and grinding hardship was, in some seasons of the year, the lot of most. Recurrent epidemics scourged alike our cities and our frontiers. A few men of industrial power could throw a region into a panic; a single person could, on a whim, shut down the mills of a community and self-righteously judge himself guiltless of the suffering imposed on the workmen and their families. The moral crime of human slavery was legalized. Millions of

65

human beings were subject to barter and sale. In 1849 we practiced democracy somewhat in the fashion of the ancient Athenian experiment and woe to him who was born of black or red skin. For him there was only the master's whip or the sword of the exterminator.

"Americans in the century just past have used the power of self-government to the progressive advantage of our people. Our fathers, and we, have fought disease, suffering, injustice, and license in all its forms so that all of us might win larger freedoms, including freedom from economic calamity with its consequences of widespread want and human misery. In doing all this we have used, whenever necessary, the government as our servant and laws as our instrument. But so far as possible, we have depended upon the force of public opinion, without direct government intervention, to bring about reform and progress—responding to our instinct that 'The best government is the least government.'

"Certainly the American Dream demands that we continue the search for betterment in the cultural and material standards of our people, using, where absolutely necessary, specific powers of law and government. Because of the complexity of the problems involved, it may be impossible for any individual to define accurately the line dividing governmental and individual responsibility in this quest. This is typical of collective activity. Two great American industries are today shut down because a few men cannot see eye to eye on specific items of employee and employer responsibility. If they—of undoubted loyalty to America—can dare calamity by their failure to agree in a far more simple decision, how can the plain citizen determine the dividing line between his own and the government's responsibilities?

"To help us, I believe that nothing could be more effective than a convocation of leaders in every field with the faculties of some of our great universities. I should be proud to see Columbia cooperating in such an effort, its purpose to develop a clear and authentic chart of this dividing line. The result might not satisfy the mind and conscience of each of us, yet the question would be rescued from the domain of prejudice, emotion, partisan politics and selfish interest and

66

be subjected to logical analysis and enlightened judgment.

"The task is to promote social and economic welfare without jeopardy to individual freedom and right. The conclusions of any such convocation would be transitory in their application, but based upon principles with which we are all familiar. The first of these is the American conviction that men are created equal; that governments are instituted to secure to man [sic] their rights to life, liberty and the pursuit of happiness. Another is the danger inherent in concentration of too much of any kind of power in too few hands.

"The leaders in our convocation would be guided also by the truth that the American Dream implies the fullest possible exploitation of American resources for the good of all. They would so locate the dividing line between government and citizen as to provide full play to the American qualities of initiative, courage, inventiveness, which, in their sum, have won us a productivity without a parallel in the world. The need for economy in government would require guards against excess of bureaus at the seat of government. Their conclusions would certainly emphasize the truth, 'More and more bureaus, more and more taxes, fewer and fewer producers; the final result is financial collapse and the end of freedom.'

.   .   .   .   .   .

"Our foremost need is strength, and *proof* of strength: moral, intellectual and material strength. We must cling ever more closely to the fundamentals of the American belief in human dignity and rights. So—as we consider measures designed to affect the status or the security of the workingman, we must ask these specific questions: 'Does the proposal push the worker one step closer to regimented labor? Does it ease the way to governmental control over his life and livelihood?' As we strive to devise measures intended to lessen the shocks and privations incident to old age, to sickness, to unemployment, to natural disaster, let us choose among the several proposals that which best protects our heritage of freedom."

Among the heritages of freedom in the General's view—as he has repeatedly said—is the profit system. In his Inaugural Address he had this to say on the subject:

"When shallow critics denounce the profit motive inherent in our system of private enterprise, they ignore the fact that it is an economic support of every business right we possess and that without it all rights would soon disappear."

In these words can be seen the broad outlines of Dwight Eisenhower's economic philosophy. They suggest that he considers himself, if one must again revert to the popular measurement, as an economic middle-of-the-roader. But they do not clearly show how he stands on many of the specific and grave problems facing the free-enterprise system—among them the present status of organized labor.

The General's younger brother, Milton, one of his closest confidants, once observed that Dwight's political and economic views were a little to the right of the middle of the road. He was perhaps speaking from his own viewpoint as a government official who had played a part in the Roosevelt New Deal reforms. In any case, some light is thrown on the General's attitude on several more specific questions, political and economic, by his public remarks on other occasions. These are treated in the following chapters.

CHAPTER VIII

Of Groups and Trends

"There is nothing wrong with America that
the faith, love of freedom, intelligence and
energy of her citizens cannot cure."

In the words that have been quoted in the last three chapters, Dwight Eisenhower has shown his intense faith in the soundness of the American idea, his conviction that that idea has made possible the freedom and progress the nation has enjoyed, and his optimistic outlook on the future, provided the American people continue to work together and meet their individual and collective responsibilities.

But these words have not dealt, except in a rather general way, with some very practical questions. They leave in some doubt the Eisenhower attitude toward a number of the most important tendencies in current American life and toward some of the very important groups that make up the American social and economic partnership.

To a large extent this is unavoidable. As has been noted before, General Eisenhower has always regarded himself as a military man who was doing a military job. Even after he assumed the presidency of Columbia University he was still in the army, subject to call. Although he felt more free at Columbia to express himself on social, political and economic matters than he had while he was on active duty, he still confined himself generally to subjects within his purview as the head of an educational institution, or to matters on which he felt strongly and which appeared germane to the occasion of his talk. The result is that his public utterances from the end of the war up to the beginning of 1952 undoubtedly do not cover all the issues and subjects on which he holds pronounced views. There are, however, some matters that he has dealt with in somewhat more concrete terms.

69

One of these is the present position and role of organized labor in its relationship to management and to the public as a whole.

Another concerns a number of interrelated factors that have operated in social and political fields during the past twenty years with profound effect on American life. This is an amorphous subject, hard to deal with specifically. It has to do with the vast expansion of governmental bureaucracy, power, taxing and spending which—beginning with the Roosevelt program to stabilize the economy after its 1929 tailspin and the social reforms and efforts to achieve better security for the American people that followed—was vastly enlarged by the crisis of World War II. It has to do not only with the Roosevelt New Deal but with the Truman Fair Deal aftermath.

A third concerns the danger from selfish pressure groups that have achieved great power and use it for the advancement of their group interests rather than for the common good. Connected with it is an evident lack of moral values in certain sections of government and business alike that endangers the American future.

A fourth has to do with the relationship of the federal government to higher education in this country—a matter in which the General, as president of one of the largest and most zealously independent educational institutions in the nation, had a vital interest.

A fifth concerns Eisenhower's attitude toward the largest of our minority groups, the Negro, and the General's views of the Negro's progress, his place in American society, and his future.

In attempting to interpret Eisenhower's attitude on these matters the collector of his public utterances runs the grave risk of presenting only one side of the picture because the expression of his views was limited to a relatively few occasions and because they bore on only a few aspects of the questions. But we are dealing here solely with the public record and must stand on that, realizing its limitations. In fairness, however, the reader should bear in mind the time and the particular occasion on which these views were given. For the rest, he must rely on the General's basic beliefs already set forth and make up his own mind in the light of these beliefs how Eisenhower thinks on a variety of kindred subjects.

ORGANIZED LABOR

It is apparent that Eisenhower believes that American labor and American management, despite their differences, are the component parts of a team that must work together for their own good and for the good of American society in general. Together they have achieved mightily in peace and in war. Together they can go on adding to the nation's strength and advancing its welfare if they respect each other's rights and do not forget that they are mutually dependent.

The General clearly is not one of those who deplores labor's material gains over the past half century or so. Conversely, he is not one of those who subscribes to the theory that a working man, merely because he belongs to a powerful union, should abandon the freedom, the initiative, and the duty to put his best efforts into the job that are a part of the American tradition. His social conscience and his ideas of cooperative American progress forbid the first. His own rugged individualism and belief in the rewards of initiative forbid the second.

His tribute to the part labor played in World War II and some of his thoughts about labor's role were given in his address to the Eighth Convention of the Congress of Industrial Organizations at Atlantic City, November 20, 1946. His words should be read against the background of his position as Chief of Staff of the Army and as a soldier who was voicing his sentiments as to the help labor had given the Army during the war. These are excerpts:

". . . Not only do you represent a vitally important segment of our nation, but this occasion gives me still another opportunity to pay personal tribute to the soldier-worker partnership that was so effective in bringing America victorious through a ghastly war.

. . . .

"There is no need for me to expound upon the importance of American labor to our position before the world, and to our

71

own future happiness and prosperity. Nor need I extol the benefits that have been brought to the American working people during recent decades by labor organizations. Men of my generation, familiar in their youth with the specter of insecurity that haunted many a family whose meager shelter and clothing and food depended on the father's prolonged hours of toil and sometimes miserably small pay, are living witnesses of what has been accomplished. My own work-week during the year before I entered the Army in 1911 was eighty-four hours.

"I should confess to you that my close associates in my office maintain that in thirty-five years I am still doing very little better. But I ask you, what other than a horse laugh would greet my attempt to organize a union for the benefit and advancement of brass hats?

"This progress has been possible because we live under a free system. Moreover, a practical result of this progress has been to enhance the enjoyment by the average American citizen of the rights, opportunities and freedoms which, under the Constitution, have been for a century and a half legally and properly his.

.   .   .   .

"The continuing efforts of organized labor to bring the good things of our country's production to the hands and homes of those of our own people who work at their creation call for every encouragement. As long as these efforts are in harmony with our national welfare every true citizen must applaud. A prosperous virile citizenry is both the purpose and the strength of democracy. So if the United States of America is to retain and enhance the effectiveness of its leadership in the new venture toward international harmony, we must, first of all, stand before the world as a shining ex-ample of the superior advantages of self-government—the social, economic and moral advantages. We cannot expect the world to show great interest in a cooperative international mechanism unless cooperative effort, which is the essence of our democracy, is successfully practiced in the homeland of its principal exponent. To maintain our national health, all groups that make up our nation must be united in their willingness to give and take for the common good."

Nearly three years later he spoke again on labor and management. He had been in this country during the intervening months, he had watched and listened, and his ideas were further developed, though not essentially changed. Both labor and management have their rights and their place, but their cooperation is essential. In the previous chapter an excerpt has been given from his address at the American Bar Association meeting at St. Louis in September, 1949. Here is another excerpt on labor, ending with a tribute to the vital importance of education in protecting labor's gains:

"Labor Day, itself, poses an immediate challenge. In every state of the Union, this day is set aside to honor the men and women who in factories and shops, in transportation and communication, in all the technical areas of our economy, have wrought the material marvel of our time—Industrial America. By their labor—teamed with the know-how of management and the vision of investors—they have produced a wealth of goods and aids to human existence, widely distributed and possessed beyond precedent in history or parallel anywhere.

"Because of our productivity and our insistence upon fairness in human relations, we have largely—though not wholly—freed ourselves from the tragic contrast of abject pauperism lying in the shadow of gluttonous luxury. That appalling picture could not be, and never will be, long tolerated by a people who believe in the dignity of man and the legitimate aspirations of all men.

"And, let us not forget, our freedom from degrading pauperism is due to America's deep-seated sense of fair play translated into adequate law; to American industrial initiative and courage; to the genius of the American scientist and engineer; and to the sweat, the organizing ability and the product of American labor in a competitive economy. It is *not* the result of political legerdemain or crackpot fantasies of reward without effort, harvests without planting.

"Acknowledged and glaring errors of the past, committed

73

by those who prided themselves as leaders of great industrial empires, have at times justified and compelled drastic action for the preservation of the laborer's dignity—for the welfare of himself and his family.

.   .   .   .

"American workingmen are principals in the three-member team of capital, management, labor. Never have they regarded themselves as a servile class that could attain freedom only through destruction of the industrial economy. With only rare exceptions, they have striven within the framework of our laws and tradition to improve their lot through increased production that profited all Americans.

"To the achievements of organized labor, my four brothers and I—all of us present at this meeting—can testify, remembering the 84-hour week and skimpy wages of our youth. But we likewise remember with gratitude the opportunities presented to us by the American environment—opportunities so rich, so profuse that we scarcely were aware that the circumstances in which we lived could be classed only as meager. Among these opportunities is that of Education.

"By promoting literacy and understanding, our schools have made it impossible for a specially privileged leisure class to prey on those who work. By opening the sciences and professions to all our people, our colleges and universities have destroyed the curse of inherited caste and made our society the most fluid yet attained by man. Though the time has not yet arrived when all men will, as a matter of course, begin their careers in the lowest positions, and from there go upward in accordance with their individual value to society, yet this opportunity today spreads itself before every intelligent, educated and energetic workman of America."

THE GOVERNMENT AND THE INDIVIDUAL

How General Eisenhower feels about the sum of the great body of social measures which since 1933 have tended to lessen differences in material wealth and improve the lot of the common man in America has been indicated only in such general terms as have already been set forth. Like many citizens, he doubtless approves of some measures, disapproves of others.

His remarks to the C.I.O., quoted in the previous section, show rather clearly that he approves, for example, as part of a continuing process of economic betterment, the gains labor has made in shortened work hours and better pay since the hard old days. But he has also stressed on many occasions his conviction that social gains achieved through government intervention must always be measured against the possible threat to individual liberties implicit in government's growing power. In general, it would seem that he thinks some of the things done under F.D.R. were good, but that others have now gone far enough, if not too far.

As an individualist and a self-made man he has shown impatience with the growing stress on security rather than opportunity. As the President of Columbia University he put his views succinctly in a speech in Galveston, Texas, when he said:

"If all that Americans want is security, then they can go to prison. They'll have enough to eat, a bed and a roof over their heads. But if an American wants to preserve his dignity and his equality as a human being, he must not bow his neck to any dictatorial government. . . . We owe it to ourselves to understand the nature of the times and not trade the principles that made this nation great for some panaceas dished out by a bureaucrat sitting in an easy chair in Washington."

In speaking to a Columbia College Forum on Democracy, attended by preparatory and high school students in February, 1949, he used his own boyhood attitude to illustrate the same theme:

"I was of a big family of boys, six of us. And we were very poor, but the point is we didn't know we were poor, and that's the point I want to make with you. The mere fact that we didn't do all the things that others in cities may have done made no impression upon us whatsoever because there was constantly held out in front of us by every one around us, and certainly it was embedded in our consciousness, that opportunity was on every side.

75

"In those days we didn't hear so much about the word security, personal security through life from the cradle to the grave, some kind of assurance that we were not going to have to go out with a tin cup or sell apples on the streets. But there was constantly around us the right and the opportunity to go out and do better for ourselves than merely to follow the plow down through the field, or to work on the section gang, or anything else that we might do to make the extra few dollars in the summer that we needed."

At the opening exercises of Columbia's academic year in September, 1949, he again voiced his belief that "security" deadens initiative:

"In these times we hear so much of security, security for everything we do—when so many of us want to be sure that we shall never be cold, or hungry, or out in the rain, or have a leaky roof—I must tell you that you have come to the wrong place if you are seeking complete fulfillment of any ambition that deals with perfect security. In fact, I am quite certain that the human being could not continue to exist if he had perfect security. I should think that the best example of it would be a man serving a lifetime in a federal prison.

"But you are going to meet here at every turn, every day, all the time, opportunity. You are going to meet it by rubbing elbows with distinguished scholars in the faculty, and among your own student body, and from them you will learn, and you will grow in understanding, and you will grow to love the fight that opportunity brings. And I hope that by the end of the year and more especially by the end of the course, the word 'opportunity' will be one that you nail to the masthead of your lifetime flag and follow forever.

"So Columbia, in attempting to make you welcome, simply says: Here, we believe, is opportunity for those who seek it, and if you enjoy your opportunities to the full you will have a lifetime of satisfaction and value to your nation, to yourself, and to your God."

Earlier that year his profound distrust of statism, on which he has been quoted in earlier chapters, was again revealed in connection with security. At the Columbia College Forum on Democracy in February, 1949, he said:

"Because the kind of dictatorship under which we may fall today is not that brought off by means of a coup d'etat and a suddenly seized power using the army or the navy and its guns to put us all in strait jackets. There is a kind of dictatorship that can come about through a creeping paralysis of thought—readiness to accept paternalistic measures from the government, and those paternalistic measures are accompanied by a surrender of our own responsibilities and, therefore, a surrender of our own thought over our own lives and our own right to exercise our vote in dictating the policies of this country. If we allow this constant drift toward centralized bureaucratic government to continue, finally it will be expressed not only in the practice of laying down the rules and laws for governing each of us in his daily actions to ensure that we do not take unfair advantage of our comrades and other citizens, but finally it will be in the actual field of operation. There'll be a swarming of bureaucrats over the land. Ownership of property will gradually drift into that central government and finally you have to have dictatorship as the only means of operating such a huge and great organization.

"I believe it is things such as that that we must watch today if we are going to be true to the standards that Lincoln gave to all of us."

There is one social reform Eisenhower favors beyond doubt —that of halting the growth of bureaucracy in government and the encroachment of the federal government on local powers and duties and on the lives of the citizens. He made this plain in the following passage from his Commencement Address at Columbia on June 1, 1949:

"Millions of us, today, seem to fear that individual freedom is leading us toward social chaos; that individual opportunity has forever disappeared; that no person can have rightful title to property; that we have reached the point where the individual is far too small to cope with his circumstances; that his lifelong physical security against every risk is all that matters.

77

More than this, we hear that such security must be attained by surrendering to centralized control the management of our society. In short, to these fearful men, the free human individual is a social anachronism.

"On every count the fearful men are wrong. More than ever before, in our country, this is the age of the individual. Endowed with the accumulated knowledge of centuries, armed with all the instruments of modern science, he is still assured personal freedom and wide avenues of expression so that he may win for himself, his family and his country greater material comfort, ease and happiness; greater spiritual satisfaction and contentment.

"When even the rudiments of knowledge were possessed by only a privileged few, when man's appalling ignorance handicapped his participation in government, there was ground to believe that an all-powerful state had to rule each subject's life from the cradle to the grave. That ground has diminished with each year of our Republic's existence.

.   .   .   .

"The modern preachers of the paternalistic state permit themselves to be intimidated by circumstances. Blinding themselves to the inevitable growth of despotism, they—craven-like—seek, through government, assurance that they can forever count upon a full stomach and warm cloak or—perhaps—the sinister-minded among them think, by playing upon our fears, to become the masters of our lives."

The growing burden of taxation is an aspect of the paternalistic state that worried him. In a speech at Fort Worth on December 15, 1949, he asked:

"How far can a government go in taxing away property rights and still not leave the government the master of the people instead of their servant?"

The extravagance and waste that may so easily accompany the expansion of government and its power over the dollars and the lives of the people is another danger against which Eisenhower has frequently warned. An example of his atti-

78

tude toward this phase of statism is seen in the following passage from his Founders Day Address at the Carnegie Institute in Pittsburgh, on October 19, 1950:

". . . If the times demand a sudden and tremendous increase in the budget for defense, reckless extravagance, selfish grabbing, heedless spending of dollars we do not possess will make American citizenship in the future a mortgaged existence rather than a joyous privilege. If solvency and security are not synonymous, they are so closely related that the difference, if any, is scarcely discernible."

We do not know from his formal speeches precisely how the General stands on some other phases of this subject of the government and the individual—among them the controversial Truman Civil Rights program. But it is safe to assume that in most cases involving the increase of power by the central government he is a states'-rights man, or at least a local-government man. He recognizes the necessity, in these dangerous times, for the individual to give up some of his rights to the central government for the sake of survival as a free individual, but he wants no jot of individualism abandoned for any other reason.

TERMITES OF DEMOCRACY

Dwight Eisenhower sees great danger to the ideals and the future of American democracy in the selfish materialism and the decline of moral standards in public and private life which seem concomitants of the present materialistic era. His attitude stems not only from his sense of moral values and his devotion to duty, but also from his fear of the destructive effects of disunity on the American way of life.

He has expressed himself strongly on the subject of pressure groups—those powerful interests which more and more amid the complexities of Big Government and the inertia of the citizen have influenced government policies for their own ends, and often against the interests of the general public. He has also blasted the mountebanks, the purveyors of political and economic cure-alls who mislead the people for their own purposes.

79

In one of his early addresses, broadcast from Germany, where he was still on active duty, to the New York *Herald Tribune* Forum in October, 1946, he foreshadowed his later more complete views on this matter. He said:

"The international respect we now have . . . can be weakened and even destroyed if at home we permit our fundamental unity to be torn apart by pressure groups and selfish factions. The respect of others, and, therefore, our influence toward peace, will likewise be lost if we should now retreat from stout defense of the ideals for which we fought the war. Never must we become so weak in any of all of these moral, military and industrial factors by which the world measures national vitality, that our ideals must be abandoned, our obligations unfulfilled and our peaceful efforts flaunted."

He returned to the subject in his inaugural address at Columbia on October 12, 1948, when he spoke not only against pressure groups but also false prophets and demagogues who arouse tensions in the American democracy. He said:

". . . It is not enough merely to realize how freedom has been won. Essential also is it that we be ever alert to all threats to that freedom. Easy to recognize is the threat from without. Easy too is it to see the threat of those who advocate its destruction from within. Less easy is it to see the dangers that arise from our own failure to analyze and understand the implications of various economic, social, and political movements among ourselves.

"Thus, one danger arises from too great a concentration of power in the hands of any individual or group: The power of concentrated finance, the power of selfish pressure groups, the power of any class organized in opposition to the whole— any one of these, when allowed to dominate, is fully capable of destroying individual freedom as is power concentrated in the political head of the state.

.   .   .   .

"There are internal dangers that require eternal vigilance if they are to be avoided. If we permit extremes of wealth for a few and enduring poverty for many, we shall create social explosiveness and a demand for revolutionary change. If we do not eliminate selfish abuse of power by any one group, we can be certain that equally selfish retaliation by other groups will ensue. Never must we forget that ready cooperation in the solution of human problems is the only sure way to avoid forced governmental intervention.

.   .   .   .

"It was loss of unity through demagogic appeals to class selfishness, greed, and hate that Macaulay, the English historian, feared would lead to the extinction of our democratic form of government. More than ninety years ago he wrote of these fears to the American historian, H. S. Randall. In a letter of May 23, 1857 he said, 'when a society has entered on this downward progress, either civilization or liberty must perish. Either some Caesar or Napoleon will seize the reins of government with a strong hand; or your republic will be as fearfully plundered and laid waste by barbarians in the Twentieth Century as the Roman Empire was in the Fifth; —with this difference, that the Huns and Vandals who ravaged the Roman Empire came from without, and that your Huns and Vandals will have been engendered within your own country by your own institutions.'"

The same theme occurred again in the Columbia Commencement Address in June, 1949:

". . . The impact on us of every international fact and crisis is immediate. We are seldom free from anxiety as each day's events crowd instantly upon our attention. Pressure groups often pretend to a moral purpose that examination proves to be false. The vote-seeker rarely hesitates to appeal to all that is selfish in humankind. Ruthless individuals, whether they classify themselves as capitalists, spokesmen of labor, social reformers or politicians, glibly promise us prosperity for our support of their personal but carefully concealed ambitions. False teachers, who magnify acknowledged errors in the practice of democracy, attempt to destroy our faith in man's right to self-government. As we seek to conserve what is good and sound even while we boldly explore and test new ways,

we are belabored by the demagogues of right and left; both
of whom would turn back the clock of history to the days of
regimented humanity. In such a maelstrom of facts and crises
and false counsel, the guideposts to individual duty and
action become obscured."

But with all his misgivings about the efforts of these ter-
mites of democracy to destroy the American Dream, Dwight
Eisenhower the optimist has faith in the ultimate capacity of
the educated and informed American to make his own judg-
ments as between the false and the true. His faith in continued progress, despite such tendencies, is shown in the
following passage from his Commencement Address, Columbia, directed at the young men and women of the graduating
class, in June, 1950:

". . . No one man can, within a single lifetime, become
fully conversant with all the skills and disciplines that bear
upon currently critical questions. None, by himself, can reach
wise answers in all. Consequently, you are fortunate in your
continuing claim upon the advice of those who have been
your teachers in Columbia. But though these selfless, patriotic
and dedicated men and women can bring to you counsel—
out of wisdom won through study and reflection—the solving
of these problems becomes, with each passing day, more and
more squarely up to you.

"It is well that this is so. Each generation fortunately brings
to its own affairs the freshness that is youth. Most profoundly
do I believe that your attitude toward human differences in
race, in color and in creed is far more generous, far more
understanding, than that in which I and my generation were
raised. Constantly re-appearing questions involving minori-
ties, discrimination, persecutions—all these will be answered
better by people who have grown up with them than by those
who, looking backward, try to fit the circumstances of today
into the patterns that they themselves knew when their own
world was young. Your decisions in these matters, which are
essentially moral,—in that they involve rights and justice and
decency more than they involve material values—will measure the conscience of your generation. Thereby, you will determine whether the world grows loftier and nobler in spirit,

or whether it turns toward cynicism, immorality, and self-indulgence. And in this determination alone is probably the real answer to most of the world's troubles; for without constantly improving standards in personal, political and economic morality, standards reflecting an indestructible faith in the Almighty, any other advance will be transitory, if not illusory."

Nowhere has General Eisenhower commented more specifically on the current effects in Washington of pressure-group influence and its effect in spurring inflation—against the warnings of President Truman. Nowhere has he commented more specifically on the results of moral let-down in public office. For the past year he has been in Europe bolstering the defenses of the free world. His position has again been that of a military man. Whatever concerns he may have had about farm and business lobbies—and about mink coats and dubious government contracts—have been unspoken. From the record one may guess that he has been deeply concerned. One may also guess that if an Eisenhower were in the position of a Truman, the chiseler in high office would have very short shrift.

GOVERNMENT AND EDUCATION

One more example of Eisenhower's attitude toward government aid—or interference—in the lives of American citizens deserves note. It has to do with education, which was close to his heart long before he became the president of a university.

As the leader of several million young Americans who fought for their country on European battlefields, he apparently approved of the educational opportunities afforded these veterans under the G.I. Bill of Rights, which involved expenses paid for by the federal government. He had this to say to the student GI's in a radio address delivered in July, 1948:

"You veterans have fought in defense of human freedom—you will be especially watchful that it is never imperiled, either from external attack or from creeping paralysis from within. In many countries you have seen the effects of governmental seizure of all property, industry, and activity including educational institutions, and you will never permit us so to enslave ourselves. You know the value of cooperation—you will struggle to see that our domestic problems are settled on that basis. You have witnessed the destruction, the suffering, the stupidity of war. You will do every honorable thing to see that global war does not again engulf us and the world. You will maintain the integrated national strength that will discourage any from attacking us, while you work unceasingly for the growth of international understanding that will eliminate war."

On the other hand, his distrust of statism and governmental interference made him feel very strongly on the question of government aid to colleges and universities if that government aid involved any interference or control over the individual institution. A direct grant of funds from the federal government would, as he saw it, have strings attached to it, unlike aid to the veterans, where, in addition, the period of time was limited. He expressed his views forcibly in an address at Albany when he received a degree of doctor of laws from the Board of Regents of the University of the State of New York in October, 1948:

"Because I believe that the Federal Government has no right to take tax money out of our pockets and give it back to us without some form of supervision, therefore I say that they cannot give Federal money for the support of higher education. When Federal money comes into that field we are entering a dangerous situation.

"So that no one will misunderstand where an old soldier stands on that question—I will have no Federal money in higher education as long as there is one single iota of Federal control coming with it."

A few months later, in June, 1949, he again clearly defined his stand in a letter replying to one from Representative Ralph Gwinn, of New York, who had asked for his advice on a proposal for new federal aid to education:

". . . Unless we are careful, even the great and necessary educational processes in our country will become yet another vehicle by which the believers in paternalism, if not outright socialism, will gain still additional power for the Federal Government.

". . . Very frankly, the army of persons who urge greater and greater centralization of authority and greater and greater dependence upon the Federal Treasury are really more dangerous to our form of government than any external threat that can possibly be arrayed against us.

". . . In such areas [those where there is need for assistance in providing proper education] I would heartily support Federal aid under formulas that would permit no abuse, no direct interference of the Federal authority in educational processes . . . I would flatly oppose any grant by the Federal Government to all states in the union for educational purposes. Such policy would create an ambition—almost a requirement—to spend money freely under the impulse of competition with other localities in the country. It would completely defeat the watchful economy that comes about through local supervision over local expenditures of local revenues.

". . . The completely spurious argument is frequently advanced that because the Federal Government skims off so much of the available tax revenue it must, as a consequence, bear more of the local expenditure. This is putting the cart before the horse. If local communities do their job then there will be no need for additional centralized revenues for nationwide subsidies of an essentially local character; and we will avoid the certain pitfalls of extreme centralization."

THE NEGRO IN AMERICAN SOCIETY

In the American melting pot one of the most difficult of all social problems has been the status of the American Negro, who constitutes a racial minority that is a component part of American democracy. The Negro's present place in the social and economic scheme of things and his future prospects are questions that have aroused great emotional reaction—both among Negroes and among whites, regardless of which side of the argument the latter takes.

Eisenhower's remarks on the subject indicate that he has great admiration for the extraordinary progress of the Negro toward full participation in all the advantages and responsibilities of American democracy and that he believes the goal will be attained. But he seems to agree with the "gradualist" theory of one of the great leaders of the Negro race, Booker T. Washington, rather than with more impatient Negro leaders who advocate the quick and violent reforms which so often cause an equally violent and opposite reaction.

At a press conference in Paris shortly after the German surrender, he was asked to comment on the contribution of Negro soldiers to the European war. He pointed out that he did not differentiate among soldiers—"I do not say white soldiers, or Negro soldiers, and I do not say American or British soldiers"—but he added that Negro units had done their duty. At the time Negro soldiers served only in Negro units, as they had done in the regular army for many years. This policy has since been changed.

The question of the Negro in the army arose at a time when Paul Robeson, the famous singer who had been welcomed in Russia as a representative of the downtrodden Negro masses of America, had been broadcasting over the Soviet radio. General Eisenhower was asked to testify before the House Committee on Un-American Activities as to the conduct of Negro troops. He said that he had previously testified about the loyalty, devotion to duty and endurance of American troops. "In that testimony," he said, "I have never made any exception based upon racial derivation or connection. I have not done so because no such exception was applicable or justified."

It was in a speech made at the dedication of a boys' building at the Harlem branch of the Y.M.C.A. in New York, on September 25, 1949, that he stated his views of the Negro's position in American life and of the agitators who seek to undermine the Negro's progress by stirring racial hatreds. He said:

". . . My congratulations and felicitations to the boys who are going to have the great opportunity of using this building and to the groups that have made it possible. Because to my mind, it is Americanism at its best.

"These people who would have us forsake the ancient principles, who would have us forego some of our liberties and our freedoms in return for what they call security from the Federal Government, are aided and abetted by a type of person called the agitator. He hopes, through the unrest that he can engender through class warfare—racial differences, to create a division that will allow him to get into a position of power where he, and his groups like him, can tell us what to do. One of the groups that the agitator is always attacking is the Negro section of the population. To my mind one of the greatest glories of the American Negro today is that this agitator has had no slightest measure of success. In my mind, not so great a success as he has had in other groups. It has been my great privilege more than once to appear before Congressional Committees, and elsewhere, and testify to the loyalty and the value to us of that great ten per cent of our population that is Negro in race.

"They, like their white brothers, have their representatives lying under the crosses of Tunisia, of Normandy, and the Rhine. They have never hesitated to spill their blood for this great country.

"It is not for any man to say today that any of us have erased from our hearts the last vestiges of prejudice. That is not true. We are a fallible people and although we may have been created in the image of our Maker, we certainly have not, at this time of world development, attained to that spiritual perfection that we can claim the virtue that we know the Creator possesses. But we can strive toward it, and what I am trying to say is the virtue in the striving.

"That is the reason that I think you should be so proud of Booker T. Washington—the man we heard so eloquently described today—Dr. Anderson; Dr. Carver; Dr. Bunche, today one of the greatest statesmen this country has produced. And I assure you I admire Jackie Robinson right along with them.

But more than that—more than in those mere special cases, I should like to point one thing out which I fervently believe —that there is no race in the history of man—none—going back to the Pharaohs and the Ark—that has, in eighty-five years, come so far on the road to understanding useful citizenship, satisfaction in its own culture, and its own advancement, as the American Negro race.

.   .   .   .

"Now if you have come all that way in eighty-five years, in terms of history, think of what great moment that is. If you will cast your minds back, how many of you here can quickly tell how many years there were, for example, between the Peloponnesian War and the Phoenician War in Rome? Well, a couple of hundred years. What I am trying to point out, ladies and gentlemen, when you look at it in terms of history, two hundred years is nothing. But in eighty-five years you have come that far. Wouldn't it be fun to cast our minds just this far forward—say when the boys, the young boys who are just going into that building—are as old as I am. Well, it's going to be about the year 2000. (Sounds like a long time when you say it that way.) They will be up here, probably with another renovation of this building and extension, a building bigger and better than ever. What will they be saying about the Negro race? I rather doubt, ladies and gentlemen, at that time if it will occur to us to mention those words. We will just say Americans, because that is what we all are. And if this great country, with those institutions to keep you and me free; that allows us to do as we please; to take a job where we want to; to think what we please; to worship as we please is going to endure, then we must practice democracy, which means that we are all merely, but proudly, Americans."

PART III

Guarding the American Ideal

"It is obvious that an enduring, world-wide and secure peace must be founded on justice, opportunity and freedom for all men of good will; be maintained in a climate of international understanding and cooperation; be free from militaristic menace; and be supported by an accepted and respected police power representing all nations."

CHAPTER IX

War and Peace

"The earth may become a flowering garden or a sterile desert—and we may make the difference."

"Peace is more the product of our day-to-day living than of a spectacular program, intermittently executed."

For an understanding of General Eisenhower's estimate of the tremendously difficult problems which confront the American system at this point in world history, the approach he would take to their solution, and his fundamental optimism that they will be solved, his own words serve better than an interpretive preface. This excerpt from President Eisenhower's Commencement Address at Columbia on June 6, 1950, epitomizes his views on the danger of war, the need to work by every means for peace, and the necessity to keep America strong in war or peace:

"World revolution, of which one objective is the elimination of the American system of government, is the announced purpose of powerful forces. But this threat is a no greater danger to the future of our mode of life than would be an accumulation of erroneous answers to currently perplexing questions.

.   .   .   .   .   .

"For none of these questions is there a pat and simple answer, even though the perennial office seeker unceasingly attempts to convince us that his own glib promises provide exceptions to this rule. The honest man must face the fact that panaceas offered us are more often characterized by surface appeal than by deep-seated logic.

"Moreover, by their nature, most of these questions will never be wholly and perfectly answered. But, unless there is constant progress toward solution that is in keeping with the essentials of the American free system, the whole order of things as we know it will pass, and those who come after you will live in a world we of today would never recognize. They could lose the free choice of religion, of occupation and of dwelling place. They would not venerate the same values, respect the same historical figures or even live under the same spiritual and political concepts as prevail today. Educational institutions would, here, as they have in some other places, become mere propaganda machines; libraries would provide priceless treasures for bonfires.

"But tragic as these developments would be, there is no reason to grow hysterical or to despair, if we are alert and determined. In the international arena, where complete isolation would be eventual suicide, we have loyal allies; even the least among them is not to be written off. Indeed, if, with them all, we can reach stronger and stronger unity of effort and dedication, based upon common standards of decency and deep-seated aspirations, confidence in peace can be gradually revitalized, and the greatest fear of mankind steadily reduced. At home, we possess broad acres, a wealth

BASEBALL—Ike (seated, fourth from left) as a member (fielder) of the Abilene High School team of 1909. Brother Edgar is at extreme right.

MARRIAGE—Lieutenant Eisenhower and Mamie Doud were married a year after he left West Point.

International News Photos

THE FAMILY—At a reunion in 1926: Father David, Milton, Mother·Ida, seated; (above) Dwight, far left, and his four other brothers.

Wide World Photos

THE BROTHERS—Twenty years later the surviving Eisenhowers met again. Left to right, Milton, Dwight, Earl, Arthur and Edgar.

International News Photos

FUTURE VICTORS—In 1933 Major Eisenhower was picked to assist General Douglas MacArthur, Chief of Staff.

International News Photos

PRELUDE TO WAR—After Philippine service, Ike and Mamie relax at a 1939 Fort Lewis barbecue.

U.S. Army Photograph

TEST OF BATTLE—Ike grins happily after the mop-up in North Africa, at a conference in Algiers (June, 1943) with Chief of Staff, General George Marshall.

STRATEGIST—The General
thoughtfully studied his maps.

SUPREME COMMANDER—Early in 1944, when he was named
to lead the invasion of France, Ike outlined to the press problems of "Operation Overlord."

D-DAY—One of Dwight Eisenhower's great decisions was the timing, against adverse weather conditions, of the invasion of Normandy. Here he is seen in England talking to paratroopers who were to form the spearhead of the attack.

MATER FAMILIAS—A wartime picture of the General's mother. She
died in 1946 at the age of 84.

HOMECOMING—The war over, Ike happily returned
to familiar scenes. This is his boyhood home.

CIVILIAN—Five-star General Dwight Eisenhower when he retired in 1948 as Chief of Staff after thirty-seven years of active duty.

THE EDUCATOR—The Eisenhower magnetism in a new setting; Ike became President of Columbia University in 1948.

HONORS—This French award was one of many presented to Eisenhower during his time at Columbia.

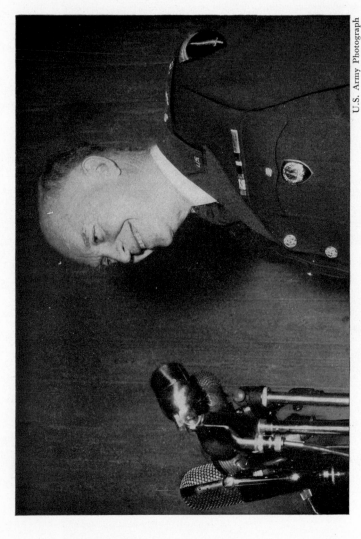

CALL OF DUTY—Back in uniform to build Europe's defenses, Ike is once more "The General."

INTERLUDE—Christmas, 1950, on the eve of Eisenhower's new service in Europe, was spent happily with Mamie in Denver.

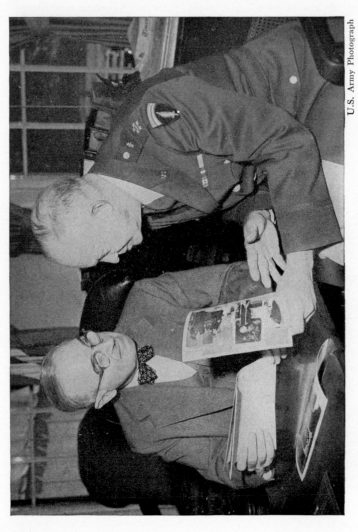

U.S. Army Photograph

NON-POLITICAL—The General and President Truman at a meeting in November, 1951, which aroused much speculation. Here they appear to be discussing the recent visit of the British royal couple, Elizabeth and Philip, to Washington.

N.A.T.O. COMMANDER—Ike inspects men of the 28th Division as they arrive in Germany to bolster Western strength.

THIRD GENERATION—The proud General
with his grandson, Dwight David Eisenhower,
2nd, aged 3.

REUNION—On a quick trip home the Eisenhowers are met by
their son, John, a major at Fort Knox, and his family.

RETROSPECT—The wartime commander, once more serving his country, thoughtfully surveys, 7 years after D-Day, the Normandy beaches where his troops made history.

This news photograph, made in 1949 as the General returned from a Florida vacation, conveys the qualities of the Eisenhower character that have won the confidence and respect of the free world.

of resources, a mighty material strength, a high level of professional attainment and general culture. These rightly used, in conformity with the great vision of the Republic's founders, can raise ever higher the standards of living and culture which have already made America unique among the nations."

ON WAR

The General's "non-military" viewpoint concerning democracy and the place of the military man in democratic society has already been examined to some extent. But the attitude of this professional warrior toward war itself has not. It may be well to look at it.

His viewpoint has much in common with that of another great and wise commander, Robert E. Lee, who, at the scene of one of his victories, remarked: "It is well that war should be so terrible; if it were not we might become too fond of it." Eisenhower, like Lee, has no love of war.

On one occasion General Eisenhower said, "I hate war as only a soldier who has lived it can, as only one who has seen its brutality, its futility, its stupidity." On another he said, "War is the least acceptable solution of our problems." On a third he said, "When people speak to you about a preventive war, you tell them to go and fight it. After my experience, I have come to hate war. War settles nothing."

He stated the same conviction in an address at Pittsburgh in October, 1950, when he said: "Possibly my hatred of war blinds me so that I cannot comprehend the arguments that its advocates adduce. But, in my opinion, there is no such thing as a preventive war. Although this suggestion is repeatedly made, no one has yet explained how war prevents war. Nor has anyone been able to explain away the fact that war begets conditions that beget further war."

His feelings about war—and with them the belief that world peace can and must be achieved—were expressed much earlier, in the full flush of victory in his address to the Joint Session of Congress on his return from Europe on June 18, 1945. He said:

"The battlefront and the home front; together we have found the victory! But even the banners of triumph cannot hide from our sight the sacrifices in which victory has been bought. The hard task of a commander is to send men into battle knowing some of them—often many—must be killed or wounded in order that necessary missions may be achieved.

"It is a soul-killing task! My sorrow is not only for the fine young lives lost or broken, but it is equally for the parents, the wives and the friends who have been bereaved. The price they pay is possibly the greatest. The blackness of their grief can be relieved only by the faith that all this shall not happen again! Because I feel this so deeply I hope you will let me attempt to express a thought that I believe is today imbedded deep in the hearts of all fighting men.

"It is this. The soldier knows how grim and black was the outlook for the Allies in 1941 and '42. He is fully aware of the magnificent way the United Nations responded to the threat. To his mind the problems of peace can be no more difficult than the one you had to solve more than three years ago, and which, in one battle area, has been brought to a successful conclusion. He knows that in war the threat of separate annihilation tends to hold allies together; he hopes we can find in peace a nobler incentive to produce the same unity.

"He passionately believes that, with the same determination, the same optimistic resolution and the same mutual consideration among Allies that marshaled in Europe forces capable of crushing what had been the greatest war machine of history, the problems of peace can and must be met. He sees the United Nations strong but considerate; humane and understanding leaders in the world to preserve the peace he is winning."

A few months later General Eisenhower, then back in Germany, spoke of the increasing destructiveness of modern war and of the necessity for the retention of American strength in order to prevent an even greater holocaust than World War II. In a broadcast to the New York *Herald Tribune* Forum in October, 1945, he said:

"As has been so clearly demonstrated at least twice within our lifetime, modern war is an all-inclusive business. It is no longer a thing apart from the core of a nation's life, a mere contest between professional warriors.

"It involves every last shred of moral and physical power that the nation can bring to bear. In our present state of development any country, no matter how wealthy, that faces the possibility of war with nothing but professional forces upon which to depend, will either bankrupt itself in the effort to sustain respectable strength, or will be so pitifully weak that the people can experience no sense of security behind it. Moreover, if a nation persists in this error a predatory power will feel freer to leap to sudden attack with less fear of the consequences. In the training of our healthy man power, as an obligation to the nation and to the individual himself, is to be found the most efficient, economical and democratic method of equalizing the burden of providing security and of standing before the world as a nation ready to defend democracy. And if any man fears that such training glorifies or promotes militarism—let him sample the mass opinion of our returning veterans. I assure you they want no more war!

"Thus we may be strong, within the means we can afford: and the words of the strong are weighty in the councils of peace. With confidence in ourselves, with consideration for the viewpoint of others, with readiness to seek acceptable solutions in those cases where our interests conflict with others, we can cooperate in the concrete problems, of which the German is only one, and we will be a vast influence in support of international law and order.

"More specifically, we will be helping to lift from the hearts and minds of our own children that age-old curse, the fear of war!"

ON WORKING FOR PEACE

That Eisenhower was clearly aware of the strenuous efforts and of the means necessary to assure peace was made evident rather early in the cold war the Kremlin has waged against the American system during the last six years. In April, 1946, at a time when many Americans were complacently assuming that international difficulties could be resolved by frank talk around a conference table, he had this to say in an address before the American Newspaper Publishers' Association in New York:

"Progress toward universal and enduring peace, as I see it, lies along three roads—organized international cooperation, mutual international understanding and progressive international disarmament. All must be traveled simultaneously.

"The first path, that of organized international cooperation, is under survey by the United Nations. That organization must have our active support, a support as tireless and effective as that which sustained our vast fighting forces through more than four years of bitter conflict. The United Nations eventually must guarantee, both to major and small powers, security against unwarranted infringement of national rights—a common cause of war.

"In this hemisphere we, with the other independent nations of the Americas, have worked out relationships in which mutual cooperation for the solution of common problems is the keynote. We live by the axiom that arbitration is a more effective means of settling disputes than is war. Years of development have been necessary to attain our present position, and while perfection has not been attained our degree of success is proof of the possibilities on a global scale.

"Progress along the second path—mutual international understanding—is of particular significance because each of us, as individuals, can contribute it. My own war experience with numerous allies convinced me of one fundamental truth in human relations—that mutual knowledge tends to eliminate mutual fear, suspicion and prejudice, the prolific breeding grounds of dissension and quarrels. Through every means open to us, we must strive for comprehension of the history, the problems and the aspirations of others, just as we must assist others to gain similar comprehension of ourselves.

"Vast gulfs of social, economic and political differences still separate the peoples of the earth. Centuries and generations have gone into their development. We cannot expect to bridge them by wishful thinking or to abolish them in a few conferences.

"Again, our own conception of democracy, no matter how earnestly venerated by ourselves, is of little importance to men whose immediate concern is the preservation of physical life. With famine and starvation the lot of half the world, food is of far more current importance to them than are political ideas. The degree of our sacrifice in feeding the hungry is the degree of our understanding of the world today. And by our conduct toward the hungry now, our country and its institutions will not only be judged tomorrow, but our own progress toward a peaceful world will be measured.

"To return to the issue of political understanding: time and again Americans have proved their readiness to fight and die in defense of certain basic principles of life and freedom. Obviously others, adhering to different philosophies, can be quite as ready to fight and die in defense of their convictions. As we make gains in mutual understanding, there will inevitably follow greater mutual tolerance in composing those differences that so often loom importantly in the more material fields of finance, trade and territory—sources of international conflicts.

"Here I think it important to remember that we can be firm without being offensive in support of principles that are sacred to us. We must realize that good humor, patience and tolerance are as important internationally as they are individually. While Lincoln's house could not stand, if divided, we know that two houses differently constructed can exist on the same street. Good neighbors do not pry into the domestic life of each other's families even while they observe common standards of conduct in their daily association. A people whose entire history is steeped in different doctrine may give to such words as democracy and freedom a totally different meaning than do we.

"Progress along this path, it seems to me, should be a particular concern of the newspaper world. Here, I think, there is for you gentlemen both an opportunity and a challenge. No single group can do more to facilitate progress along the road of mutual understanding than those who direct the publicity media of the world.

"The third path to enduring peace—progressive international disarmament—is the one that engages the soldier's special attention. To believe that uncoordinated disarmament can liberate us from fear of war is a fatuous notion, as the files

95

of the American newspaper bear witness. In World War II, four great nations paid a ghastly price for failure to preserve coordination. For France the result was Hitler's jig in Compiègne forest. For Britain it was Dunkirk. For Russia it was the long and bloody retreat to Stalingrad. For us it was Bataan and Corregidor.

"On the record, uncoordinated disarmament by itself is a treacherous road toward our goal. The caution to be observed is that disarmament is not unbalanced. But this truth does not lessen the importance of insisting upon progressive, universal disarmament. The results will be universally beneficial. First, the resources now poured into organizations whose purposes are essentially negative and sterile will be devoted to the constructive purposes of peace. But more than this—the effect of progress along this path will engender mutual confidence and so promote a more rapid movement along the two others. That progress will, in turn, permit further disarmament. Thus there will develop a reciprocal effect that will hasten full attainment of the ultimate goal."

A little more than a year later he followed up these thoughts with a speech which, directed to his immediate audience, likened the effort by men of good will to control war to the cooperative effort man has made to cope with the natural disasters that have always threatened his possessions and his existence. Talking to a meeting of the National Board of Fire Underwriters on May 27, 1947, he said:

"We realize that calamity is a part of human life so long as men through carelessness, stupidity, ignorance or criminal intent breach the barriers against it, but we do not relax our effort to make its penalties less severe on the innocent. Although our tribute during the past twelve months to the god of fire cost hundreds of millions in dollars and more than ten thousand lives, we do not accept such losses as inevitable, if men are prudent and alert. Fire, famine, pestilence consequently have lost much of their ancient terrors as the scourges of human existence. We recognize their remaining threat as largely the penalty of our indifference or neglect.

"War, however, is not a natural evil; it is man made. Combining all the horrors of the other three, its malevolence and diabolical savagery has been increased by man himself in the very years that he has learned control over the natural evils of life. As never before, the essence of war is fire, famine and pestilence. They contribute to its outbreak; they are among its weapons; they become its consequences. The tragedy of war is multiplied by acceptance of its inevitability, although since man is its origin—his carelessness, stupidity or criminal intent the occasion of war—it should be subject to the same prevention and control as the evils that comprise it.

·   ·   ·   ·   ·   ·

"Citizen, community and nation joined to help defeat the menace of fire. . . . There is here the shadowy outline, at least, of a pattern of effort against war! For too many generations, too much of the world has taken it for granted that war is a normal part of human life, whose penalities can be lessened, not by rooting out the cause of war, but only by maintaining so large and powerful a war machine that defeat would be impossible—the equivalent, say, of maintaining fire departments on every street corner or building cities of tinder and tissue.

"As I see it, we need an organized effort, embracing every phase of society, whose goal will be the development of individual, community and national attitudes that will remove war from the category of the inevitable into its proper position as an evil subject to prevention, or at least control.

·   ·   ·   ·   ·   ·

"In the effort toward international safeguards, we shall not work alone. Nations now are seeking, at the highest level, to develop cooperation and arbitration as a barrier against war. There is no people that does not hope for their success in this attempt. If we lead the way in showing how this international endeavor may be reinforced and supported all the way back to the individual citizen, we shall not lack for followers. Regardless of his race, politics or creed, the common man, when given a worthy goal and guidance toward it, does not rest until it has been attained.

"In a world of independent nations, where men comprehend the causes of war and understand their mutual responsibility to control them, war may happen—but it will cease to be an institution, a characteristic of human society.

"The stake in the campaign is not property and dollars, no matter how wasteful war is of these commodities. It is not merely famine and pestilence for a given proportion of the earth's population. It is, rather, the way of life to which we are devoted; it is civilization as we know it. Even more, it is rapidly becoming humanity's existence."

Eisenhower has much more to say on the prevention of war and on how he thinks the foreign policy of the United States can be directed to that end. He also has more to say on the United Nations and the part the cooperation of the free countries can play in assuring world peace. But for the moment let us turn our attention to another factor in the Eisenhower thinking—his views as a military leader on the capacities of the American to defend his way of life and on the organization of the nation's military forces for preparedness against possible attack.

CHAPTER X

The Military Defense of America

"Until the day when the United Nations can guarantee our international security, we ourselves must assure our national security. But our security program, if it is to be a bulwark of democracy, must be the concern of every citizen and not merely the vocation of a small professional group."

The Congress of the United States and the people of the nation have frequently heard General Eisenhower's views on military matters. It is the one subject above all others on which he is qualified by training and personal experience to give counsel. It is one on which he has full right, and indeed obligation, while in uniform, to speak when called upon. This was especially so during his service as Chief of Staff from late 1945 to April, 1948, when he had the task of transforming the Army from a wartime to a peacetime basis. During that period he frequently testified before Congressional committees on the status and needs of the armed forces.

At the start, it is obvious that the General believes 100 per cent in military preparedness to defend the values of life this country cherishes. On at least two occasions he has quoted St. Luke (11:21–22):

"When a strong man armed keepeth his palace, his goods are in peace: But when a stronger than he shall come upon him, and overcome him, he taketh from him all his armour wherein he trusted, and divideth his spoils."

To examine his opinions in the military field, we may separate them into four major topics and see what he says on each. These are:

1. The qualities of the trained American fighting man.
2. The need for military preparedness.

3. Universal military training.

4. Unification of the armed forces.

On all of these questions General of the Army Dwight Eisenhower has stated pronounced and clear-cut views. His expression of these views has had much effect on subsequent measures to increase military efficiency.

THE AMERICAN SOLDIER

The General's respect for and sense of comradeship with the men of his profession has often been shown. It was eloquently stated in his final Order to the Troops on his retirement as Chief of Staff to become the president of Columbia University:

"Departure today from my present post breaks many ties that are dear to me. But the separation is not complete. I take with me the knowledge that, both by law and in my heart, my service with you shall not end as long as I live. Assurance of such fellowship is my most prized possession, for no man can have a more worthy comrade and loyal friend than the American soldier."

On the place of the soldier in American society and on his duty to the nation, the General said, in a speech at West Point in June, 1947:

"Your immediate mission is one upon which the very existence of our nation may depend—the fortress [of freedom] must be strong, its garrison the embodiment of military effectiveness.

"But this service does not imply subscription to the rule of might. War is mankind's most tragic and stupid folly; to seek or advise its deliberate provocation is a black crime against all men. Though you follow the trade of the warrior, you do so in the spirit of Washington—not of Genghis Khan."

What Eisenhower thinks of the courage, the individual initiative and the general capabilities of the American soldier when he is well trained and well led have been put on the record many times. One example, from his address before the joint session of Congress on his return from Europe in June, 1945, will suffice to show how he feels:

"I have seen the American proved on the battlegrounds of Africa and Europe over which armies have been fighting for more than two thousand years of recorded history. None of those battlefields has seen a more worthy soldier than the trained American."

MILITARY PREPAREDNESS

As commander of the American occupation forces in Germany and later as Chief of Staff, Eisenhower saw, and was concerned about, the politically potent "get-the-boys-home" movement which brought rapid demobilization of what was perhaps the most powerful army in history. It had popular backing; it stemmed from the dislike by most Americans of peacetime military life; but it had grave effects on American strength in a world which, for all its momentarily bright prospects after Allied victory, was far from peaceful, as events proved. Eisenhower warned of the dangers of too great demobilization. In a report before a special meeting of Congress in January, 1946, he put the problem in simple terms:

"You see firemen playing checkers sometimes," he said, "but that doesn't mean you fire them and send them home. They may be vitally needed a few minutes later.

"It's the same way with our occupation forces. We must maintain them at a safe level, because we may need them, even though we don't have full work for all of them, all the time."

He went on to say:

"I know and you know, that many of them [the soldiers on occupation duty abroad] are homesick men. But there is a job to be finished. Although our allies are carrying a heavy load, Americans have assumed the definite commitment and responsibility of carrying out their own share. To the Army

101

has been delegated the principal job in performing this work. The work cannot be done without men. Remember, this is your Army—not the War Department's Army and not the General's Army. It belongs to the country—to the Congress and the people. It carries out their wishes and their orders."

With prophetic foresight he added:

"When we have secured the peace and liquidated our emergency tasks, we shall then have a third task—to preserve the peace. This is the long-term, continuing peacetime mission of the Army. It will be the job of our permanent peacetime military establishment. The size and composition of that establishment are, of course, up to you."

Ten months later, with Soviet obstructionism becoming more evident, he had this to say about preparedness in an address broadcast to the New York *Herald Tribune* Forum:

"Great tragedies do not spring out of logic and reason. We found in 1914 and again in 1939 that abuse of power, lack of restraint in its exercise, lust for its increase breed war. We learned that though the world's masses may recoil from the thought of war, wherever they are regimented, inarticulate or tragically misinformed, a mere miscalculation by a few officials of another's intent or strength can result in conflict. In many regions, local passions, misguided fanatics and age-old prejudices can all bring about crises of the gravest kind. "The world organization is striving to develop machinery to control such dangerous outcroppings of human weakness and greed for power. Until that has been accomplished, demagoguery, fed on fear and hatred, can still bring misery to millions of weary people. While this situation endures, we must realistically face the need for military strength adequate to our times and our position. Every American, as well as the Army, owes first allegiance to our country. No crime could be greater than blind exposure of America's heritage to ruthless attack, merely because we hate war with a consuming hatred. To work for peace does not excuse you, or the Army, from the toil and work of assuring our own security."

He again urged that Americans prepare for defense on a realistic and democratic basis which would enable the marshaling of their forces quickly in case of need without dangerous disruption of their liberties and their economy. In his speech to the American Newspaper Publishers' Association in April, 1946, he said:

"National security, as I see it, is a state of organized readiness to meet external aggression by a quick and effective mobilization of public opinion, trained men, proved weapons, and essential industries, integrated into the most efficient instrument of armed defense, and reinforced by the support of every citizen in the measure and form necessary for the preservation of our way of life.

"The security establishment comprises all the people, all our enterprises, all our Government if it is to be adequate in this atomic age. But it must so engage their efforts as to permit the full development of every aspect of peaceful life.

"The security establishment of our democracy must always remain representative of our way of life. It must not be a belligerent and noisy horde, screaming threats of atomic destruction, disrupting world harmony. It must not attempt to build the country into a warehouse or stockpile for war. Belligerence is the hallmark of insecurity—the secure nation does not need threat to maintain its position.

"Moreover, there is no guarantee of security in military machines alone—twice in our lifetime we have broken the most powerful military machine in Europe and, during the latest war, we reduced its Pacific counterpart to a huge but helpless skeleton.

"In the final analysis, whether or not the Army can do its part for democracy depends on the citizen's interest in the service and, reciprocally on the army's understanding of its relations with the citizen. The American newspaper can bridge the gap that has too often separated them in the past."

In an address before the Industrial Associations meeting in Chicago in January, 1947, he showed concern over American complacency about the atom bomb as a defense against Soviet aggression. He referred to it as a counterpart of the

"Maginot Line mentality," which had done so much to destroy France in 1940. He warned against postwar apathy. He said:

"The time interval between initial assault and a crippled nation has been narrowed by every improvement in offensive weapons. . . . An incontestable conclusion that emerges from World War II is that modern wars are fought with the concerted strength of whole nations, and that the integration of our national economy into an effective security machine must be accomplished—in thought and in plans—before an emergency occurs. The responsibility for achieving this purpose rests with all of us in solving the problem."

Against the background of a growing demand for economy in government expenditures for defense and of mounting danger in the "cold war," he sought to strike a balance between the two in a speech which recognized the need to economize by cutting wasteful spending but also pointed out that America's defenselessness in previous times of crisis had cost many times the amount that would have been spent on keeping an adequate military establishment. In an address at a civic reception in St. Louis in February, 1947, he said:

"No sane American, aware of the world's need for our stabilizing influence, denies the essential role of armed strength for our own security and for the maintenance of peace. The important question is, how much, for likewise no one denies the crying need for economy. Neither of these conflicting requirements can be ignored; in every military activity and project they must be considered together.

"Economy, insofar as it confines expenditures to essentials and requires thrifty and careful administration, is always necessary, whether we are concerned with the management of a household, or city or army. For example, a profusion of military posts, once necessary for the protection of pioneers, should now be consolidated in the interests of economical administration and professional efficiency. Every army activity should be held under a critical eye to determine that satisfaction of national needs does not provide excuse for indulgence in careless spending. There is no risk or danger in such economy. Quite the contrary; but neither is there any economy in military nakedness. Time and again we have proved the staggering extravagance of penny-wise policies."

UNIVERSAL MILITARY TRAINING

On this highly controversial question General Eisenhower early took definite stand. He was for it, both as a democratic principle and as a practical necessity.

In a letter from Supreme Headquarters dated June 2, 1945, and released at a hearing of the House Special Committee on Post-War Military Policy, later in that month, he said:

"Fairness to the country and the individual's chances of survival in war demand that each able-bodied citizen receive in time of peace a thorough grounding in technique, discipline and understanding of the citizen's obligations in time of emergency.

". . . To realize the possible purpose of speediest possible mobilization of maximum power, after an emergency, much of this training must be done in peace. Physical hardening will always have to be repeated after the war starts, but takes the least time. Technical training takes more time, but with individuals graduating from a full course of training before the emergency starts, units with competent leaders will quickly qualify for service. . . . There is no possibility of overemphasizing the value of intelligent training of this kind."

Eisenhower knows from his own experience at West Point and in the army that military training does not tend to make a robot or a slave of the free individual. As he said to the convention of the Congress of Industrial Organizations at Atlantic City in November, 1946:

"I do not want to leave unchallenged the bugaboo so often used by ignorance or prejudice, that military training results in harm to the individual. The records of every university in the land demonstrate the contrary. Not only are veterans proving the natural leaders of their classes, scholastically also they are establishing a record whose excellence amazes every experienced educator. The average man benefits from military training and should there be raised the old bogey of 'regimentation of the mind,' I ask you to look at the veterans among your own ranks to see whether you can find any evidence. In this regard I offer as the first exhibit the committee that met me. If you think they are regimented you talk to them. The average veteran has developed in leadership, in initiative, in mental maturity and in self-reliance by reason of his service. The medical check-up and the physical hardening incident to his duty are positive assets. He is a better citizen because he has borne his part in defending all citizens, and because he did so in a crisis that demanded full play for the best of man's virtues."

Earlier, in November, 1945, he had this to say on the subject in testimony before the House Military Affairs Committee:

"We must be prepared on M-day—the day the enemy strikes—or we may never be prepared to avert defeat at the hands of any aggressor who uses against us the weapons of the future. Our weapons must be better than theirs on that day, our resources must be promptly available and above all our manpower must have already been trained. This training must be given in time of peace. Without a standing army of prohibitive size this can be accomplished by training our civilian reserve, our citizen army. The most democratic way to do this is by universal military training, in which every able-bodied young man is fitted to discharge his duty to protect our freedom. This has been the ultimate solution in every major military crisis this country has faced. The only difference now, and the great lesson of World War II, is that it must be done before not after the first shot is fired.

.   .   .   .

"I believe that every combat leader in our armed forces agrees that success is possible only when the mass of the army is composed of the younger men. They are more readily adaptable to combat conditions and possess more vigor and dash. Certainly, the technical services must comprehend a high proportion of younger men who are capable of mastering the radically new techniques of future warfare. Therefore, it is a matter of necessity as well as fairness to add increments of currently trained young men to the civilian reserve. The alternatives are the criminal sacrifice of untrained young men, or calling on unfair proportions of older men who have already done their duty. In either event we would be without the services of trained technical specialists who will only be found among the younger men.

.   .   .   .   .   .

"This is our greatest assurance of keeping the peace for which we fought. Far from being contrary to the purposes and intent of the United Nations Organization, I consider it to be essential to the success of that organization. I know of no better or more democratic way to demonstrate our willingness and ability than to adopt now a program of universal military training. It is eminently fair to our citizen army who fought and won this war in two ways: First, it is the best way of assuring them that they did not fight in vain; second, it will relieve them in the shortest possible time of continuing to bear the burden, as the current trained civilian reserve, of defending the peace.

"Gentlemen, I have heard many arguments about the desirability or undesirability of universal military service from a moral, educational and religious standpoint. These factors have always been of the greatest concern to me in the discharge of my functions of command. There is no question but that the sum-total of these values makes up the very essence of the thing we fought to preserve—our American way of life. But the facts of today must be faced. The preservation of our way of life in a world which twice within a single generation has fought to virtual exhaustion depends squarely upon the national security. That is a truism.

"I sincerely believe that the only practicable way to assure the national security is by peacetime military training and that this must be universal. No practicable alternative, that I have heard of, has ever been suggested. Therefore, I believe arguments as to the incidental disadvantages or benefits to be foreign to the main issue. I feel completely confident that the Congress can provide all the necessary safeguards to prevent abuses of a method forced upon us by a necessity which must be faced.

"I feel sure that no true American would be willing to take on his own shoulders the awful responsibility for actively prohibiting all training and thus leaving our country defenseless and naked before a future enemy armed with the weapons of that day. But our fighting forces in war are always made up of civilians, so a failure to provide for the training of the civilian reserve amounts to nothing less than condemning us to such a state of helplessness. A large standing Army would certainly be much more objectionable on all of those grounds even if it were not economically impossible to maintain one of sufficient size without impoverishing the country.

"An aspect of this whole problem that deeply concerns me is that of the rights and the best interests of the young men destined to receive the training. I wonder whether any honest opponent of peacetime training has any clear conception of the difference between the trained and untrained men on the battlefield? In terms of the larger issue of victory or defeat comparison is scarcely possible, because in modern war it is not possible to win without training. But in the more personal matter of the individual's chances for survival I should say that the trained combat soldier has at least three times the chances of the untrained to live to become a veteran!

"I have sincerely searched my mind on this whole problem! Through the past three and a half years the picture of the progressive destruction of civilization which war brings was constantly before me. I keenly felt the burden of the terrible responsibility I bore. I shuddered particularly at the thought how close our own beloved country came to being afflicted with the same devastation and our own people with the same indescribable sufferings that came to the peoples of Europe. I know that if it had not been for the time given us by the almost superhuman efforts of our Allies, we would not have been able to mobilize our resources or to train our men to avert disaster.

"I know that the nature of the weapons available to future

108

aggressors makes it ridiculous to hope that we will somehow miraculously be given this same time again. Our resources must be already available, our weapons must be second to none in speed and effectiveness. This means that we must be preeminent in technical research and in industrial mobilization, and we must have a trained force large enough to make our resources and weapons instantly available for our needs.

"Thus we will be a potent power to preserve the peace, and in position to act swiftly in our own preservation if the tragedy of war again appears. I do not see how we can escape the inexorable logic of the fact that if we are to attain and maintain this reasonable and necessary position we must have a trained reserve of citizens in being. This means that we must train them in peacetime."

UNIFICATION OF THE ARMED FORCES

This was another controversial question which aroused bitter feelings among many of the traditionalists in the different branches of the military services. General Eisenhower, with his knowledge of the practical value of cooperation by different nations and different branches of the services of the different nations, and of the effect of centralized direction of these disparate groups in winning the war in Europe, was an early exponent of the unification of American military forces.

His "air-mindedness" and his observation of the part the Navy had played in the invasion of Europe perhaps motivated his thinking. At any rate, he consistently upheld the idea of unification in the postwar arguments on the question. Without doubt, the weight of his judgment had much to do with the eventual decision to make the American fighting services a single, hard-striking force.

While the war was still going on in the Pacific he had this to say about unification in a Paris press conference in June, 1945:

"There is no such thing as a separate 'air' war, as a separate 'ground' war, or as a separate 'sea' war or 'logistic' war or any other branch.

"Great nations determine the political purposes of war. The

Governments determine the general areas in which they choose to apply their tactical power, and then they begin to make resources ready of the general nature needed; they turn the problem over to a commander and his staff and subordinate commanders, and they fill out the resources on the recommendations of those people in the field who have a chance to study the problem at very close range.

"But in all cases it is the integration of all types of those powers and forms of war that bring you your answer in the quickest possible way.

"It is perfectly true that your air, for example, has to wipe the other fellow's air off the earth before he can go ahead and use his full power in an offensive way. That is merely the job he does in order to do his main task of advancing your own cause. When you put sea, ground and air together, the result you get is not the sum of their separate powers. You multiply their power rather than add.

"The whole basis of thought that led to the attack across the Channel was this: That air power in overwhelming strength applied to a particular area could paralyze traffic, could immobilize the enemy, could soften up his defenses, could make possible operations that would otherwise be and remain in the realm of the fantastic."

In May, 1947, he told another Congressional Committee:

"In this day of scientific and technological war it is of primary importance to balance the security forces against world conditions as they exist from year to year. The establishment of single responsibility and authority for submitting recommendations to the President and to Congress, and for carrying out the mandates of the Congress will constantly bring to our ever changing problems, involving the three services, solutions applicable to the time and conditions.

"Without such single direction we tend to become compartmented into fixed forms and practices that grow more rigid with time.

"I emphatically support the principle of providing a single civilian head of the armed forces, one who may give his entire attention to this vital phase of the nation's affairs."

110

CHAPTER XI

Education—Weapon of Democracy

"Love of freedom, confidence in cooperative effort, optimism, faith in the American
way will live so long as our schools loyally
devote themselves to truly liberal education."

Education, or lack of it, shapes adult convictions. It is likely
also to shape the future of the world. What, then, are General
Eisenhower's ideas on education?

They are broad. He believes that education should not
merely be a means of acquiring knowledge or specialized
techniques that will enable the individual to make his way
in life, but also should inculcate moral values, and develop
character and an awareness of one's duties as a member of
democratic society. It should also—and this is significant of
Eisenhower's thinking as an educator—enable the student
as an individual in a free society to examine and weigh all
the cultural ideas and values that have marked the record of
man's progress, and help him to choose between the false
and the true.

Eisenhower believes in a free education that allows full
freedom of expression. Against the indoctrinated youth movements of totalitarianism, with their substitution of slogans
and mass emotion for thinking, he would oppose a tough-
minded youth whose intelligence has been whetted in the
clash of ideas. The Communist as a teacher is not to be
trusted; he is a propagandist of a false doctrine, not an objective examiner of the truth. On the other hand, Eisenhower
does not join in the witch hunts for teachers who present to
their students the history of Communism as one of the facts
of human history that should be recognized.

As he said in his Inaugural Address at Columbia University,

111

to be quoted later: "The facts of communism . . . shall be taught here. . . . The truth about communism is, today, an indispensable requirement if the true values of our democratic system are to be properly assessed." There must be free inquiry—but not under communist guidance. He would not appoint a known communist to the faculty—but, as a matter of academic freedom, he is opposed to special loyalty oaths for faculty members. In an Associated Press interview in New York in August, 1950, he said:

"Before appointing a man to our faculty, I would want to know all there is to know about his background. If I found he was a Communist, I would not appoint him. On the other hand, I certainly do not believe our faculty members should be subjected to special loyalty oaths.

"When we think of the education of our youth, we think of three institutions: the family, the church, and the school. We don't ask for special oaths from the parents; we don't ask for special oaths from the minister; then why ask for a special loyalty oath from the teacher?"

As we have seen, he is opposed to aid from the federal government to educational institutions if that involves federal control in any degree. In a letter to the alumni of Columbia in February, 1949, he wrote:

"A dictatorial government cannot abide free universities as America understands them. Hitler's Germany found it necessary to replace regular teachers with men controlled by a central government, who were told what they were to teach. . . . The United States . . . can remain free and can maintain the freedoms of the individual American only if it trains succeeding generations of youth in more effective citizenship."

Our schools have the opportunity, and the obligation, to develop better citizens, which will bring about greater national unity, as he said in his broadcast "The Veteran Wants to Know," in July, 1948:

112

"When veterans speak of national strength they do not mean only tanks and planes and ships. They mean the combined moral, intellectual, economic and military strength of our 140,000,000 people. The cornerstone of that strength is an essential unity among us. Without unified and concerted action no military unit, no industry, no nation can exert, either for good or evil, the full measure of its power. But whereas in some countries this concerted action is achieved by the police power of the central government, the American system repudiates every suggestion of central dictatorial control. This means that in our country, basic unity must come from a common knowledge and understanding of the critical problems of our time. To help promote such knowledge and understanding is the fundamental mission of educational institutions. Every school, from kindergarten to the greatest universities, such as Columbia, must remain true to this purpose if it is to be of the fullest service to our nation. Of course these schools are responsible for turning out the best doctors, engineers, lawyers, teachers, nurses, farmers and businessmen that can be produced. But unless our schools, above all else, strive to train America's youth for effective citizenship in a free democracy, all their other efforts will, in the end, result in failure."

These better citizens, because of their academic experience, will lead fuller, more useful and more satisfactory lives, as he told the graduating class at Columbia at the 195th Commencement Exercises in June, 1949:

"Beyond the purely academic or professional [training]—and more important to humanity—is your readiness for responsible citizenship.

"We trust that Columbia has strengthened within you the conviction that human freedom must be treasured beyond all else—even life itself—for any diminishment of it is a tragic backward step. We hope that this school has inspired within you a resolution to live the full lives of American citizens, good neighbors in every community task and in your aid to those less fortunate than yourselves; forever building a stouter team work within our people. We hope, too, you will always be sharply conscious that the great rights you possess are accompanied by inescapable obligations; that you can most surely preserve your own rights by defending the rights of others.

"And we hope that your faith has been strengthened in the wealth of opportunity our country and civilization spread before the individual; that you have grown in courage to defend the old when it is good, to move forward fearlessly on the path of proved principle, undaunted by the pitfalls to left and right—today our stark need is courageous and wise men and women, who conserve their goodly heritage while they add new richness to it."

As educated citizens the graduates of the colleges and universities of the country will be better equipped to resist the attacks of disunity within and communism from without, as Eisenhower pointed out in his Inaugural Address:

"Who among us can doubt the choice of future Americans, as between statism and freedom, if the truth concerning each be constantly held before their eyes? But if we, as adults, attempt to hide from the young the facts in this world struggle, not only will we be making a futile attempt to establish an intellectual 'iron curtain,' but we will arouse the lively suspicion that statism possesses virtues whose persuasive effect we fear.

"The truth is what we need—the full truth. Except for those few who may be using the doctrine of communism as a vehicle to personal power, the people who, in our country, accept communism's propaganda for truth are those most ignorant of its aims and practices. Enlightenment is not only a defender of our institutions, it is an aggressive force for the defeat of false ideologies."

Eisenhower sees the college graduates of the country as not only better citizens but as better leaders, who will help to guide the nation not only towards internal unity but towards international understanding. In an address before the American Alumni Council at Amherst College, Massachusetts, when he was awarded the Council's Award of Merit, in July, 1946, he said:

114

". . . As in all mass efforts, leadership is an essential ingredient, leadership in all walks of life, in every type of activity. No other is better suited to its exacting and important requirements than the graduate of the American college."

Even before his Columbia years he had had the same conception of the role of our educational institutions. In a talk at the Lafayette College Alumni Dinner on November 1, 1946, he outlined his views:

"It is my conviction that there is no agency or no institution of civilization that can do so much for the world today as its educational institutions, specifically its colleges, colleges that take the lead and set the pattern for our educational system. We must teach understanding and knowledge of each other. Little boys are afraid of the dark, and we are afraid of the unknown. I cheerfully and promptly admit there are conditions in the world today that make the attempt to exchange information and understanding a most difficult procedure. But whenever the educator or the leader in any walk of life becomes discouraged in front of the difficulties, the rebuffs (sometimes he considers them insults), let him remember to think of the problem in the terms of its terrible alternatives. . . . in this great business the colleges must teach us not only how to be skillful in our own professions, how to make more money than if we had not come to college. They must teach us how to live. The world needs to know how to live—how to live together."

Leading the nation to a better understanding of world problems is only one of the many opportunities that open before the college graduates of today. He enlarged on this theme of opportunity in an address at the orientation meeting of the freshman class at Columbia on December 5, 1950:

"All of you people should allow no bleakness, no brisk danger in the world today to make you divert one iota from the path of education which you have laid out for yourselves.
"At the very, very best most of your lives will be lived in a period of tension, a high level of tension which will force you

to accommodate yourself to a good deal in your homes and everything you do that none of the rest of us have had to face. The boyhood of people like me seems almost carefree compared to what the young men of today can look forward to. This means that you as a generation, earlier than most, should be prepared to take over, and should insist on taking over, as soon as you can, and if this is a decade of decision you are the people who are going to have to execute the decisions. Older people have some experience, if it has been experience and not merely endurance, and may be able to give you guides, principles, basic truths; you should heed those well, but do not be bound by any procedures, any application of those principles to your problems because all your lives you are going to have to live with them.

．　　　．　　　．　　　．　　　．

"You have the God-given privilege of devoting your lives to those things which you deem important. By your determination to live freely, your determination to make certain that everybody around you is living freely (remember your own freedom is in danger if you deny freedom to others), if your lives as well as your preaching are devoted to the ideal of living freely and making it possible for a nation to live freely and to give you and to maintain for you the rights to do that —that is your problem, and you can do it.

．　　　．　　　．　　　．　　　．

"How does man wrest the greatest happiness out of life? All of us will sooner or later come to realize that there must be some spiritual satisfaction that enters into the whole concept of real contentment and happiness. That you can gain and have the greater opportunity to gain. You have one special opportunity—you have a hard problem to solve and if you do it right you can certainly proudly say 'I am a citizen of a free country.'"

But it was in his Inaugural Address at Columbia University, on October 12, 1948, that Eisenhower expressed himself most fully on the important subject of the values and goals of education:

"The educational system . . . can scarcely impose any logical limit upon its functions and responsibilities in preparing students for a life of social usefulness and individual satisfaction. The academic range must involve the entire material, intellectual, and spiritual aspects of life.

.   .   .   .   .   .

"That day [when either civilization or liberty must perish] shall never come if in our educational system we help our students gain a true understanding of our society, of the need for balance between individual desires and the general welfare, and of the imperative requirement that every citizen participate intelligently and effectively in democratic affairs. The broadest possible citizen understanding and responsibility is as necessary in our complex society as was mere literacy before the industrial revolution.

"It follows, then, that every institution built by free men, including great universities, must be first of all concerned with the preservation and further development of human freedom—despite any contrary philosophy, or force that may be pitted against it.

"At all levels of education, we must be constantly watchful that our schools do not become so engrossed in techniques, great varieties of fractionalized courses, highly specialized knowledge, and the size of their physical plant as to forget the principal purpose of education itself—to prepare the student for an effective personal and social life in a free society. From the school at the crossroads to a university as great as Columbia, general education for citizenship must be the common and first purpose of them all.

"I do not suggest less emphasis on pure research or on vocational or professional training; nor am I by any means suggesting that curricula should be reduced to the classical education of the nineteenth century. But I deeply believe that all of us must demand of our schools more emphasis on those fundamentals that make our free society what it is and that assure it boundless increase in the future if we comprehend and apply them.

"Love of freedom, confidence in the efficacy of cooperative effort, optimism for the future, invincible conviction that the

117

American way of life yields the greatest human values—to help the student build these attitudes not out of indoctrination but out of genuine understanding, may seem to some to be education in the obvious.

"Of course, the reverse is true. There is a growing doubt among our people that democracy is able to cope with the social and economic trials that lie ahead. Among some is a stark fear that our way of life may succumb to the combined effects of creeping paralysis from within and aggressive assault from without.

"Fear of the future with a concomitant sense of insecurity and doubt of the validity of fundamental principles is a terrible development in American life—almost incredible in the immediate aftermath of America's most magnificent physical and spiritual triumphs. Only by education in the apparently obvious can doubt and fear be resolved.

"Here lies a heavy obligation on Columbia University and all her sister schools; unless such fear is banished from our thinking, the sequel will be either the heavy curse of tyrannical regimentation or the collapse of our democratic civilization in social anarchy.

.   .   .   .

"Historical failures in the application of democratic principles must be as earnestly studied as the most brilliant of democracy's triumphs. But underlying all must be the clear conviction that the principles themselves have timeless validity. Dependence by the country upon the schools for this vital service implies no infringement of academic freedom.

"Indeed, academic freedom is nothing more than specific application of the freedoms inherent in the American way of life. It follows that to protect academic freedom, the teacher must support the sum total of the principles which, among other things, guarantees freedom for all. The teacher's obligation to seek and speak the truth is further safeguarded by university custom and commitment.

"There will be no administrative suppression or distortion of any subject that merits a place in this University's curricula. The facts of communism, for instance, shall be taught here—its ideological development, its political methods, its economic effects, its probable course in the future. The truth about communism is, today, an indispensable requirement if the true values of our democratic system are to be properly assessed. Ignorance of communism, fascism, or any other police-state philosophy is far more dangerous than ignorance of the most virulent disease."

CHAPTER XII

The Citizen—His Rights and Duties

"The rights we have today we may consider as natural rights, but they were won by blood, sweat, sacrifice and death."

Along with military defense and the building of character and cooperation by education, there are two other components that are important in the preservation of our democracy, as Eisenhower sees the matter. One of these is the proper exercise of the rights and duties of citizenship by all members of our free cooperative American society. The other is the preservation of the freedom of speech and of the press, which are among the fundamental rights guaranteed to Americans under the Constitution.

CITIZENSHIP

The theme of the responsibilities of citizenship runs through many of General Eisenhower's talks. He feels that we cannot be reminded too often that our freedoms were won against immeasurable difficulties by our forefathers and must be retained by the same sacrifices if necessary. The General sees a good citizen as a responsible man of integrity, a patriot devoted to his country, watchful of his government's actions, informed about domestic and foreign affairs, and intelligent in his appraisal of panaceas offered to cure national and international ills.

In one of his early talks, the address at the Freedom House Anniversary Dinner, which was broadcast from Germany, on October 7, 1945, he said in connection with the promise of the peaceful future that the United Nations charter holds for the world: "We, as citizens, cannot shift our responsibilities

120

to the shoulders of representatives sitting around a conference table. We must strive for understanding and be ready to do our part in substituting cooperation for conflict."

A little later, before the Bureau of Advertising of the American Newspaper Publishers' Association, in April, 1946, he said: "Intelligent familiarity with our military problems is as essential to good citizenship as is knowledge of public schools or public finance. . . . Free institutions confer on each of us priceless privileges, but with an equal obligation to defend them. . . ."

In his Inaugural Address at Columbia University, in October, 1948, he defined what he meant by citizenship:

"The common responsibility of all Americans is to become effective, helpful participants in a way of life that blends and harmonizes the fiercely competitive demands of the individual and of society. The individual must be free, able to develop to the utmost of his ability, employing all opportunities that confront him for his own and his family's welfare; otherwise he is merely a cog in a machine. The society must be stable, assured against violent upheaval and revolution; otherwise it is nothing but a temporary truce with chaos. But freedom for the individual must never degenerate into the brutish struggle for survival that we call barbarism. Neither must the stability of society ever degenerate into the enchained servitude of the masses that we call statism.

"Only when each individual, while seeking to develop his own talents and further his own good, at the same time protects his fellows against injury and cooperates with them for the common betterment—only then is the fullness of orderly, civilized life possible to the millions of men who live within a free nation.

"The citizenship, which enables us to enjoy this fullness, is our most priceless heritage. By our possession and wise use of it, we enjoy freedom of body, intellect, and spirit, and in addition material richness beyond the boast of Babylon. To insure its perpetuation and proper use is the first function of our educational system.

"To blend, without coercion, the individual good and the common good is the essence of citizenship in a free country.

121

This is truly an art whose principles must be learned. Like the other arts, perfection in its manifold details can never be attained. This makes it all the more necessary that its basic principles be understood in order that their application may keep pace with every change—natural, technological, social.

"Democratic citizenship is concerned with the sum total of human relations. Here at home this includes the recognition of mutual dependence for liberty, livelihood and existence of more than 140 million human beings. Moreover, since we cannot isolate ourselves as a nation from the world, citizenship must be concerned too with the ceaseless impact of the globe's two billion humans upon one another, manifested in all the multitudinous acts and hopes and fears of humanity."

In his address to the New York *Herald Tribune* Forum on October 24, 1949, he had this to say on the subject:

"In revising the governmental structure, in approving new appropriations and new governmental ventures, in reforming tax laws, in considering a multitude of glittering proposals—each of which is held by its author to promise eternal happiness and prosperity—let us hold ever before our eyes the simple truth that to men who have lived in freedom there is nothing in life so valuable as freedom—not even life itself.

"If today, we never give up the effort to determine—so far as each of us can—the probable effect of every new governmental proposal upon our personal freedom, we will be discharging one of our most acute responsibilities as American citizens. But thereafter it is still necessary to act, to use all the detailed political machinery, including the two-party system, intended to give each of us a voice in his own government. In precinct or district caucuses, in party councils, in all the ways that are open to us, we must act decisively and within the limits established by our own understanding of freedom's requirements. . . .

"Put all of this into the language of practical action and we would say to ourselves:

"Our American heritage is threatened as much by our own indifference as it is by the most unscrupulous office-seeker or by the most powerful foreign threat. The future of this Republic is in the hands of the American voter.

"And we would further advise ourselves:

"Stop shrugging off politics as only the politicians' business: stop banking on American luck to get us good government and good policy—sometime it will run out.

"Stop using the alibi, 'one vote doesn't count.' It won't, only if not used! And our neighbor's won't, unless we make him use it.

"Dishonest political promises to selfish groups—not rebuffed at the ballot box—can make a nightmare of the American Dream.

"But wise and determined performance of our civic duties can make that dream come true."

And in his talk to the Boy Scouts at Valley Forge, July 4, 1950, he summed up his conception of the patriotic citizen in two paragraphs:

"Among ourselves, we do not speak openly and frankly, as often as we should, of patriotism—love of country. It is *not* that we fear the jeering of the smart-aleck; possibly we forget that men grow in stature only as they daily rededicate themselves to a noble faith. More likely, we thoughtlessly assume our blessings of liberty to be indestructible.

"True patriotism places the public good above individual advantage. It is not tainted by false pride in might, in size, in overwhelming power; it never seeks to compel others to a blind obedience to our wishes. It is among the greatest of human virtues. Fortunate are we whose devotion is to a country that seeks the good of all its citizens without distinction, that firmly champions the cause of human rights, and offers the hand of friendship to every other nation whose purpose is peace and justice."

FREEDOM OF SPEECH AND OF THE PRESS

In his European campaigns General Eisenhower, coping with the problem of how to keep the American public informed of the progress of the war without divulging important information to the enemy, showed his deep regard for the right to free expression of opinion and the dissemination of facts to the American people. His handling of the difficult case of General Patton has already been described. On many other occasions he frankly gave the press confidential information on plans in advance of their execution, as background for their later coverage—in keeping with his beliefs in the right of free speech and his conviction that a well-informed democratic opinion is the best safeguard of democratic liberties.

During the war and afterward he frequently paid tribute to the free press of the United States and to the effort, at least by the great majority of the more responsible newspapers, to report the news fairly and objectively and to interpret its meaning so that Americans might participate intelligently in the duties of citizenship. One of his most complete statements on this subject was given before the Bureau of Advertising of the American Newspaper Publishers' Association in New York on April 25, 1946. At that time he was concerned about the tendency of the American people to forget about military security in time of peace. He said:

"The American newspaper, as a recorder of national achievements and of the counsel of our country's leaders, is a repository of much wisdom applicable to fundamental problems of today. Tonight, with that thought in mind, I go back fifty-one years to a New England newspaper reporting an 1895 Memorial Day address by a citizen-soldier whose name is now enrolled among our immortal great. He said:

"'Although the generation born about 1840, and now governing the world, has fought two at least of the greatest wars in history, and has witnessed others, war is out of fashion, and the man who commands the attention of his fellows is the man of wealth. Commerce is the great power.

"'We do not save our traditions, in this country,' he continued. 'The regiments whose battleflags were not large enough to hold the names of the battles they had fought, vanished with the surrender of Lee, although their memories inherited would have made heroes for a century. It is the more necessary to learn the lesson afresh from perils newly sought, and perhaps it is not vain for us to tell the new generation what we learned in our day, and what we still believe.'

"Those are not the words of a saber-rattling brass hat. They were spoken by one of the greatest democratic figures our country has produced, the younger Oliver Wendell Holmes, three times wounded in combat as a captain of infantry, for a generation justice of the Supreme Court.

"What I must commend to you from the quotation is Holmes' stress on our widespread tendency to ignore, in time of peace, the basic military problems of our country.

"Intelligent familiarity with our military problems is as essential to good citizenship as is knowledge of public schools or public finance. In a country with twenty million war veterans—one out of every seven of our population—it should be the normal thing. But objective interest in our own military affairs has never been a peacetime characteristic of our nation.

·   ·   ·   ·   ·   ·

"Today, our generation, just as did Justice Holmes', has witnessed two terrible wars within the span of a single lifetime. Yet, in the shadow of the most costly conflict of all time, we ignore the lessons of our past history and of events daily recorded in the American newspaper. We do not see military problems clearly since they come into our range of vision only as an irritating distraction to our view of a goal that beckons brightly on the horizon of our hopes—the attainment of universal and enduring peace.

"That peace, once achieved, will eliminate the need for maintaining military establishments. And so, by wishful conversion of hope into accomplished fact, we refuse to look at the problem of today. We brush aside the long years of future trial and error and experiment and compromise, the solution of problems deep-rooted in human nature, the conquest of historic prejudices and antagonisms, all of which will be necessary to build a world cooperating for peace. An old Latin proverb counsels—'to the stars, through difficulties.' It does not deny realism in urging constancy to a vision.

"Upon my return to this country, I was confronted by an

emotional surge that was both normal and understandable. Revulsion against war was instantaneous and almost total in its scope. It was natural, and in the view of any thinking man, to be expected. Emotion has its place in the scheme of things —it is a priceless ingredient to action. However, emotion tends always to swing to the extremes of the pendulum—logic and judgment seek to find the mean between them.

"The newspaper, of course, must reflect the day-to-day attitude—even the emotions—of the people it serves. But equally the newspaper must strive to point out the path of logic. This, the bulk of our own press has never failed to do. It is doing so today. Perhaps emotion is subsiding and we are about to face reality.

"During the war you bolstered our armed strength by supporting national unity. Since the victory, the free press of America has exercised its right and its duty to criticize defects discovered in the structure of our military establishment. That was as much a part of your essential function as your wartime effort."

PART IV

America and the World

"The best foreign policy is to live our daily lives in honesty, decency, and integrity; at home, making our land a more fitting habitation for free men; and, abroad, joining with those of like mind and heart, to make the world a place where all men can dwell in peace."

CHAPTER XIII

America's Foreign Policy

"We cannot escape the responsibilities of leadership. To fulfill them, we must make clear that our interests are broad and sympathetic, that we are not worshippers of the machine, obsessed with its inanimate products, but that we are a people who view with understanding and compassion the entire field of problems affecting mankind."

General Eisenhower's international outlook and his ideas on foreign policy appear to derive directly from his beliefs in the efficacy of cooperation among people of good will when they seek to protect themselves from a common danger or to achieve a common good. In short, they are the products of his essential creed of "Americanism."

Whether he agrees with all aspects of the Truman administration's foreign policy is a question that cannot be answered definitively on the basis of his public statements—and this assessment of his thinking must stand on his public statement. But it is evident on that basis that he agrees wholeheartedly with the major portion of the decisions and actions that have constituted American policy during the first six and a half postwar years.

He approved of the effort to achieve world peace and stability through the establishment of the United Nations, which was begun under Roosevelt but formally carried out under Truman. He agreed with that most important part of Truman foreign policy which, at first directed toward efforts to get along with Russia on the basis of reason and mutual tolerance, came eventually through successive stages of disillusion to acceptance of the fact that only a determined stand could cope with Soviet imperialism. When the American people began to understand the double-dealing Soviet policy of talking peace, friendship and "co-existence" while taking advantage of every Western weakness, the American government decided to halt the enemy offensive by aid to Greece and Turkey in what was then the most critical sector of Soviet attack.

The logical extension of this policy was the Marshall Plan, initiated in 1947 for the purpose of aiding the economies of war-weakened Britain and the shattered countries of Western Europe. These nations, the original sources of the American ideas of freedom, had in the aggregate an immense productive potential which made them the chief, long-range goal of Soviet ambition. Here was the greatest danger point. The American government recognized the fact and acted to counter the threat. That General Eisenhower thoroughly agreed with this decision is proved not only by his words but by his subsequent return to active service and his highly effective work in spurring the defensive effort of the Western European allies.

On another and much more controversial aspect of the Truman administration's foreign policy he has said little that is revealing except on one important point. This phase of foreign policy has to do with Asia. More specifically, it concerns the American policy toward Nationalist China during the war and afterward—from the time General Marshall was sent to China, in December, 1945, to try to stabilize that area of Asia by composing the Nationalist-Communist differences, through the subsequent Communist conquest of China, to the present undeclared war in Korea.

Even in 1945 he distrusted Soviet intentions in China. So, five years later, he was prepared to agree with Truman's decision to oppose Communist aggression in Korea. He made this clear in a talk to the Boy Scouts at Valley Forge on July 4, 1950. He said:

"At this moment, a friendly republic suffers outrageous invasion. The South Koreans' only crime has been the desire to live their own lives as they choose, at peace with the rest of the world. The American decision to assist them was inescapable. The alternative would be another kind of Munich, with all the disastrous consequences that followed in the wake of that fatal error twelve years ago. Now, our decision must be carried to its conclusion by whatever means are necessary. In firmness for decency and readiness for any eventuality lies the only possible route to the peace and friendliness with all the world we so earnestly seek. . . ."

For one of the most complete statements on General Eisenhower's views on foreign policy we must go back three years from the Korean crisis to his speech to the American Legion convention in New York in August, 1947. His words should be read against the background of the developing international crisis and of his concern with the military defenses of America at a time when many Americans were still complacently hopeful that the desire of the peoples of the world for peace could be reached by international agreements freely negotiated and honestly kept. On the 29th he said:

"Our nation is faced today with problems, present and future, which equal in scope and significance any it has hitherto met in 171 years of existence. Because we are close to them, it is difficult to recognize their historical import. But grave they are, almost beyond precedent, and they deal—as did our great crises of the past—with the freedom of man. What America does today, what America plans for tomorrow, can decide the sort of world the generations after us will possess—whether it shall be governed by justice or enslaved by force.

"We have lately emerged from a war into which we threw

—without stint or hesitation—life, treasure and resources so that we might subdue the forces of aggression and make this earth a happier, safer place. Military victory won, we have contributed freely to the rehabilitation of stricken areas, with no regard for profit, save that which would accrue to all humanity from a stable peace.

"Mindful that world chaos is the enemy of our security, we have held out the hand of friendship to all, refraining from interference in the internal affairs of others. We have sought for all peoples the opportunity of choosing freely their form of government. Thereby we have accomplished much for humanity. Had it not been for the policy of our Government and the generosity of American men and women during the past two years, the world today would be in hopeless plight.

"Nevertheless, we find ourselves blamed, castigated, excoriated by some for any and all our efforts toward peace. In our own country, the shortsighted cry 'internationalism,' implies a lack of patriotism in those who struggle to maintain world conditions essential to the preservation of our own freedoms. Are we expected to sit idly by, doing nothing, while hunger and hopelessness inexorably push the shadow of enslavement ever and ever closer to our own shores? From without, false propaganda brands democracy a menace to progress. The exercise of the freedoms for which we fought in solemn pact is blocked in critical areas by forceful imposition of minority dictatorial control.

"In the face of such discouragement, and under the burdens that destiny has placed upon our shoulders, it grows difficult to hold the course set by our conscience. But the world is in a fluid, turbulent period and unless we continue to do our utmost to make it a better place to live, the problem will likely be how to preserve it as a place in which we can live.

"We have been witnessing a vast transfer of sovereignty from the few to the many. Three monstrous dictatorships have been overthrown and we are hopeful that in the lands of their origin the roots of democracy will take firm hold. Elsewhere, peoples who have lived in subordinate status for generations are receiving independent statehood. But, against this, nations which were free and independent members of the pre-war European family are now caught in a stifling web of circumstances, crushing independent thought and action —national or individual.

"Our Government, acutely aware of the significance of these contradictory currents, has announced its support of the first trend and its opposition to the second. The alternatives are sharply defined; the friends of freedom must stand staunchly in its support or its foes will eliminate freedom from the earth. For the United States there can be only one choice.

"Among the nations devoted to justice and freedom, destiny endows our own with the ability and capacity to assume leadership. We have the will; we have the means. Well knowing this, an enemy of freedom would, in future war, fix upon us as his first and principal target. Thus on our security depends the existence and growth of a free world.

. . . .

"But we must face the hard fact that, during the two years since hostilities ended, the cooperative spirit has lost ground. The world comprises two great camps, grouped on the one side around dictatorships which subject the individual to absolute control and, on the other, democracy which provides him a free and unlimited horizon. In my view, conflicting political theories can exist peacefully in the same world provided there is no deliberate effort on the part of either to engage in unjust coercion or unwarranted interference against the other. But as long as deliberate aggression against the rights of free men and the existence of free government may be a part of the international picture, we must be prepared for whatever this may finally mean to us.

"To work for peace and eventual disarmament, but at the same time to look well to our own security in a troubled world, is thus a central problem of the day. I ask you to remember, in what I have to say about relative, as opposed to absolute security, that I am discussing issues forced upon us by the slowness of progress toward our desired objective— the substitution of the council table for the battlefield.

"Another thing—I do not want to be understood as seeing a global war as an immediate threat. It is fully as important to prevent blind fear and hysteria from influencing us as it is to look facts soberly in the face and thus develop logical conclusions from the survey. No great nation is today in position deliberately to provoke a long and exhausting conflict with any hope of gain. But time, foresight and concerted effort are all necessary in order to possess, at any given time, a respectable defensive posture. Consequently, the subject assumes for us a critical urgency as long as the will for permanent peace has not been universally demonstrated.

"Moreover, the senseless storm of war has more than once begun its destructive course in spite of, rather than because of, deliberate intent. Any such explosion, now or in the future, must not find us unprepared. And finally—the weight of our peaceful counsel will most certainly be measured in today's circumstances, as much by the world's respect for our actual and potential strength as by our own sincerity.

"We must so gird ourselves that a predatory aggressor will be aware of the risks he runs and will realize, should he provoke war, it will likely be fought over his territory. This means that we must be ready, not only to endure and survive the first hard blows of an enemy, but to recover immediately, to strike back, to hit harder than he does—to win. All must know that we have this capacity.

"The American process of government—everything for which our people have fought and will if necessary fight again—gives a potential enemy, through the transparency of our processes, great advantages. It gives him full notice of our defensive intentions and the assurance that we will not—that we cannot—secretly plot an aggressive war. The bulk of his intelligence information is available in the public press and in the open debates and decisions of the United States Government. There is no way except through genuine preparedness by which we can convince a possible aggressor that he can choose war only at the cost of his own exhaustion or destruction.

"For the United States this means many things. It means the determination of all of our people to work together in meeting any real threat as it begins unmistakably to develop. It means unity of purpose in all issues that affect the national interest; it means an adequate force to execute the people's will; it means money to support the necessary defensive system."

Eight months later, amid the growing clash of world forces, General Eisenhower retired from active duty to become president of Columbia University. At that time he again outlined his ideas of American foreign policy in a speech which foreshadowed his later statements on the necessity for Western European unity in the defense of liberty. In his address before the Chamber of Commerce of the State of New York in May, 1948, he said:

"If we are correct in the thesis that our security forces are defending a way of life, then our attention is instantly drawn to the one thing that presents to each of us more worry today than any other. That is the seemingly inescapable, implacable contest between two ideologies in the world: the one, chiefly exemplified by ourselves, based upon human dignity and rights; the other upon statism.

"Our great concern with the other nations of the world is that recognizing the existence of that conflict—although I am one of those who sincerely believe that all our leaders and our Government tried to avoid it—we want the greatest circle of friends that it is possible for us to have in the world.

"By every man, by every nation, by every community that is added to the areas in which our form of government is practiced, and where people can practice it in prosperity and in security—by that much, we are strengthened. If that is done successfully, there can be no one that will challenge us.

. . . .

"In the European concert of Western nations where we are attempting to set up an economy that can support itself, we must never forget one thing: that they have a common security problem.

"And in your own study of that problem—which is certainly in many of its phases more profound than any I can give to it —I want to bring out one point that you may have overlooked. That is the attitude of the general staffs of the armies, of the navies, and air forces, in those separate countries. As a general staff contemplates the possibility of crisis or emergency, it wants to make sure that it has at hand those things, those raw materials, those factories, those industrial capacities that it may need in war.

"If we are going to make Western Europe an economic unity, it becomes almost certain that we must make it a political unity, or certainly a group in which each member can depend upon each other without question so far as this matter of national security is concerned. Because, if it is an economic unity, it is reasonable to suppose that leather and clothing will be made in one country: that steel goods, guns will be made in another; possibly airplanes in another. Each general staff will therefore have to depend upon the others.

"And that can be done only if alongside of any attempted economic unity is some kind of a unity that has regard for this terrific problem of national security.

"My friends that come to see me from those countries never let me forget that issue. They say: 'Yes, we want to live like the United States. But there are many reasons why we cannot get up and shout that we want to do it.' That is because there is the element of existence involved in those instances where these countries might be taken over and retire from free institutions to fall under the influence of dictatorships.

"So they must be secure, and we must not quail in helping them. Indeed, I firmly believe we must make it part of our program that we make provisions for the security of Western Europe as we invest wisely, to make them economically sufficient—so that they may make a living under a system of free enterprise.

"In like measure, although in varying degree, these same things apply to many other nations of the globe. They are matters for our Government and State Department to discuss in detail and to furnish us information on which we can make our own conclusions.

"The whole purpose of my little talk, gentlemen, has been this: To stay sane, sober, in our approach to this problem, realizing there is no temporal power on this earth equal to the aroused, unified effort of America. There is none. We need have no fear of anybody if we will stay unified behind the great principles that have made this country what it is today.

"A second purpose is to have you realize that in all of these nations today, the problem of security takes equal precedence with that one of economic recovery, and we must insist that the programs go forward hand in hand."

CHAPTER XIV

Communism—Enemy of Liberty

"As I see it, the struggle facing us today is
freedom against dictatorship under a doctrine called communism."

General Eisenhower's attitude toward Soviet Russia in the
crucial mid-months of 1945 seems to have been conditioned
by two factors. One was his duty to try to get along with the
difficult Russians in Germany in the effort to avoid friction
and reach an understanding, if possible. The other, based on
an appraisal of the military situation after the defeat of Germany and before the defeat of Japan, was a belief that concessions to the Russians to get them to join the war on Japan
were not only unnecessary but dangerous.

One of the chief evidences of this latter factor in Eisenhower's thinking comes from the diaries of that tragic figure,
Secretary of Defense James Forrestal. After a luncheon with
Eisenhower two years later, Forrestal noted that President
Truman at Potsdam, in July, 1945, had told Eisenhower that
one of his main objectives was to get Russia into the war
against Japan. Eisenhower, according to Forrestal, stated his
opinion that Japan was already beaten and begged the President not to give any important concessions to the Russians
in the Far East.

His cooperative attitude toward his Soviet opposite number in the early days of the occupation, Marshal Gregory
Zhukov, has already been indicated. But even in the com-
paratively friendly Zhukov Eisenhower found a deep Russian
suspicion and doctrinal rigidity. In his efforts to bridge the
chasm, Eisenhower used man-to-man tactics. On one occasion when Zhukov had entered into a dialectical argument of
East-West differences from the official Russian view, Eisenhower is reported to have said in effect: All right, we just

don't like your system and never will, but that doesn't prevent us from getting along together if we put our minds to it.

In August, 1945, he was an honored guest in Moscow where he talked with Stalin and other officials of the Soviet government. He returned with the impression that the Russian economy had a long way to go to repair war damages. But while in Moscow he strove to get a message through the Soviet censorship to the Russian people. It was that Russia and the United States, to be friends, should strive to understand each other, to keep a sense of values and not be led astray by propaganda.

From his experience with the Russians in Germany his recipe for dealing with them was: "Firmness, patience, a sense of humor—and keep your powder dry."

This was a tolerant and practical attitude in dealing with such an uncertainty. But as the cold war deepened, as Russia tightened her hold on the satellites of Eastern Europe in violation of solemn agreements with the West, as the Kremlin's ultimate enmity and opportunistic program to destroy Western freedom became more and more apparent, Eisenhower's attitude hardened, as did the attitude of most Americans. Russian communism had moved from the role of an ally to that of a doubtful partner to that of an active enemy. In October, 1948, the General's opinion was expressed in this excerpt from his Inaugural Address at Columbia:

"Today's challenge to freedom and to every free institution is such that none of us dares stand alone. For human freedom is today threatened by regimented statism. The threat is infinitely more than that involved in opposing ideologies. . . . democracy and the police state have no common purposes, methods or aspirations. In today's struggle, no free man, no free institution can be neutral. . . ."

Under the growing threat he had this to say a year later in his address to the *Herald Tribune* Forum:

"Under the atomic shadow, the world dwells in two hostile camps. The one is dedicated to human freedom and human rights, founded in the dignity of man. The other is committed to a dictatorship of the proletariat where the state decides

136

what rights, *what* freedom the individual may enjoy. This basic cleavage, of itself, would apparently involve no irreconcilable antagonisms. But communistic leaders openly declare that individual freedom and free enterprise, as we practice them, cannot exist in the same world with communism. They leave us no doubt on this point. In their declaration is a tragic and continuing threat to our kind of government. In view of the dynamic force with which these leaders are prosecuting their aims, we scarcely need further incentive to concentrate our thinking, our planning, and our actions toward preservation of freedom against threats from without."

The evident need to counter the barrage of hate unloosed on America by the industrious Soviet propaganda organs was noted in the General's testimony before the Senate Foreign Relations Committee in July, 1950. Eisenhower's answer was to tell the world the truth about America's intentions—and to present the truth in a more effective fashion than it had been presented. He said:

"Just recently we moved into Korea with the very best of intentions, the intention to help a people live its own life. And what has happened? Propaganda has so twisted our act as to make it appear a vicious stage in American imperialism.

"The truth can almost be classified as our T-bomb in this war. It can be won by truth. But the front on which it must be done is very broad. We need a general staff of a new kind. We can't load all the responsibility on any one department."

He advocated the establishment of a propaganda agency, the kind of work done last by the O.W.I. and the O.S.S. He said this was a special situation which should not be left to the State Department, or rather that the State Department should not be burdened with it, but that in normal peacetime the State Department should be in charge of any selling of America abroad.

This statement foreshadowed his address in Denver on September 4, 1950, which formally launched the Crusade for Freedom Movement. Eisenhower, typically, approved of this as a free-enterprise effort to convey to the world the message of Americanism unhampered by the official, diplomatic handicaps which had surrounded governmental efforts in that direction. These are excerpts from that speech:

"Americans are dying in Korea tonight. They are dying for ideals they have been taught to cherish more than life itself. But it will be written and said tonight in Warsaw, in Prague, in Moscow, that they died for American imperialism.

"Unfortunately, millions of people will believe this devilish libel against American soldiers, who have taken up arms in defense of liberty a second time in a tormented decade. Those millions will hear no other version but a hissing, hating tirade against America.

"We think it incredible that such poison be swallowed; but those people, behind and beyond the Iron Curtain, have seen so much political wickedness and cold-blooded betrayal, such godless depravity in government that they find it harder to believe in our peaceful intent and decent motives than in the calculated and clever lies that communism is spreading every hour, every day, through every broadcast and newspaper that it controls.

"This slander against our purposes and our men in Korea is merely one example of the campaign of hatred that is being waged against America and freedom around the globe. We face not only ruthless men, but also lies and misconceptions intended to rob us of our resolution and faith within, and of our friends throughout the world.

. . . .

"The Communist leaders believe that, unless they destroy our system, their own subjects, gradually gaining an understanding of the blessings and opportunities of liberty, will repudiate communism and tear its dictators from their positions of power.

"They know that, for the mass of humanity, America has come to symbolize freedom, opportunity, human happiness. They have a mortal fear that this knowledge will penetrate eventually to their own people and to all others in the world.

"Communistic aggression, inspired by fear, carries with it the venom of those who feel themselves to be inferior. This accounts for the depth of their hatred and the intensity of their thirst for power.

"To destroy human liberty and to control the world, the Communists use every conceivable weapon: subversion, bribery, corruption, military attack. Of all these, none is more insidious than propaganda. Spurred by this threat to our very existence, I speak tonight about the Crusade for Freedom.

"This crusade is a campaign sponsored by private American citizens to fight the big lie with the big truth. It is a program that has been hailed by President Truman, and others who have heard of it, as an essential step in getting the case for freedom heard by the world's multitudes.

"Powerful Communist radio stations incessantly tell the world that we Americans are physically soft and morally corrupt; that we are disunited and confused; that we are selfish and cowardly; that we have nothing to offer the world but imperialism and exploitation.

"To combat these evil broadcasts the Government has established a radio program called the Voice of America, which has brilliantly served the cause of freedom. But the Communist stations overpower it and outflank it with a daily coverage that neglects no wave length or dialect, no prejudice or local aspiration, weaving a fantastic pattern of lies and twisted fact. They confounded the listener into believing that we are warmongers; that America invaded North Korea; that a Russian invented the airplane; that the Soviets, unaided, won World War II; and that the secret police and slave camps of communism offer humanity brighter hope than do self government and free enterprise.

"We need powerful radio stations abroad, operated without governmental restrictions, to tell in vivid and convincing form about the decency and essential fairness of democracy. These stations must tell of our aspirations for peace, our hatred of war, our support of the United Nations and our constant readiness to cooperate with any and all who have these same desires.

"One such private station—Radio Free Europe—is now in operation in Western Germany. It daily brings a message of hope and encouragement to a small part of the masses of Europe.

"The Crusade for Freedom will provide for the expansion of Radio Free Europe into a network of stations. They will be given the simplest, clearest charter in the world: 'Tell the truth.' For it is certain that all the specious promises of communism to the needy, the unhappy, the frustrated, the downtrodden, cannot stand against the proven record of democracy and its day-by-day progress in the betterment of all mankind.

.   .   .   .   .   .

"In the totalitarian countries the individual has no right that the state is bound to respect. His occupation is selected by his masters, his livelihood is fixed by decree, at the minimum which will give him strength to work another day.

"Because representative labor leaders of America know the record of communism in beating down labor, they have long been in the forefront of those fighting the spread of this vicious doctrine. But communism goes further than the exploitation of labor. Unless the individual accepts governmental mastery of his life and soul, he can be convicted without trial; he can be executed without the right of appeal; he can be banished to live out his life in a slave camp.

"This is what the Soviet planners contemplate for all the world, including America.

"We must meet this threat with courage and firmness. Unless we look, with clear and understanding eyes at the world situation confronting us and meet with dynamic purposes the issues, contained therein, then we will lose the American birthright. The system of government established by our forefathers will disappear. The American record, from Washington to the day of that disaster, will be only a blank page in history.

.   .   .   .   .   .

"The die has been cast in Asia, but we are in no limited conflict. Free Europe, struggling for moral and economic recovery, is still a tempting target for predatory military force. We must give real support to all aspects of the military aid program and re-examine, at once, our troop strengths in critical areas.

140

"All this means that we must resolutely tighten our belts, both nationally and individually. We must insist upon facing up to the task of paying for the accomplishment of these vital measures, else the Soviets will take heart from their success in bringing us further inflation and closer to economic ruin.

"We must have efficiency and economy in all governmental expenditures; and we must concentrate all our resources to assure victory in this bitter and probably prolonged struggle. Until it is won we must practice spartan frugality in all non-essential matters, so that we may make the greatest possible contribution to the defense of our way of life. All lesser considerations must wait: we cannot tolerate politics as usual any more than we can tolerate business as usual. Ladies and gentlemen, we must get tough—tough with ourselves.

"Success in such national crises always requires some temporary and partial surrender of individual freedom. But the surrender must be by our specific decision, and it must be only partial and only temporary. It must be insured that, when the crisis has passed, each of us will then possess every right, every privilege, every responsibility and every authority that now resides in an American citizen. It would do no good to defend our liberties against Communistic aggression and lose them to our own greed, blindness, or shiftless reliance on bureaucracy and the Federal Treasury.

"In the dangers and trials ahead, our ultimate security lies in the dynamic purpose, the simple, courage, unshakable unity of the United States and the free world; a unity that depends upon common understanding of and common veneration of freedom. But these can live only where there is access to the truth. Thus truth becomes our most formidable weapon, a weapon that each of us can help forge through the Crusade for Freedom.

"And let us never forget that for those who have lost freedom there is no price or cost or sacrifice that can even faintly reflect its value. But it is still the core of America's boundless heritage. It will remain so for as long as we plain American citizens are ever ready to guard it with vigilance and defend it with fortitude and faith."

CHAPTER XV

Specific Questions of Foreign Policy

"Intelligent people are not isolationists."

"A nation's security in war and peace demands participation in the community of nations."

"From the beginning of time, every invention of mankind has been capable of two uses, good and evil. It is up to the moral fiber of mankind to decide to which use an invention is put. But certainly at this time, faced as we are with a Godless opponent, I do not believe we should bury our heads in the sand."

"It is possible, even probable, that hopelessness among a people can be a far more potent cause of war than greed."

These quotations exemplify Dwight Eisenhower's thinking on four specific and very important questions having to do with American foreign policy and the role of this country as the leader and mainstay of the free world. We have already seen how he feels about the Soviet menace and what he would do to combat it by building up military defenses and by a psychological counteroffensive. Let us now examine his attitude toward four problems in the international field on which there is evidently some divergence of opinion among the American people. They are:

Isolationism—or the latent tendency of some Americans to say to themselves: "It is all too much to cope with; we are not sure we can depend upon foreign allies; it would be better to let them go their own way."

World cooperation for peace—despite Soviet obstructions —through the United Nations.

Control of the atom bomb, or the H-bomb, and their use in the defense of America.

The question of *economic aid to our allies* in general and also to underdeveloped countries for the purpose of raising living standards and combating the miseries and social unrest on which communism thrives.

We have already seen a good deal of what General Eisenhower thinks on these subjects. But here are some more specific statements which leave little doubt as to his views.

ISOLATIONISM

One may venture the thought that in the background of Eisenhower's stand on this question are three chief factors. One is his fundamental belief, as a general principle, in the practical value of cooperation. Another is the record of America's failure after World War I to exercise leadership for peace that might possibly have averted World War II— a failure due to the disillusion and isolationism that followed the first world war. A third is Eisenhower's deep conviction that America must unite the free nations or risk disaster in the current struggle with Communist totalitarianism.

The type of isolationism that figures in present political thinking is not as simple a matter as the isolationism of the early 1920's. Then the oceans were still barriers to foreign aggression and the connection between the problems of Europe and Asia and those of the Western Hemisphere were not so apparent as they became a decade or so later. The isolationist of today may grant that the United States must take a much more active part in international affairs than his predecessor believed necessary. But he still has reservations about the lengths to which this country should go, particularly in certain parts of the world. Basically, he still believes that America will do best for herself by not getting too deeply involved in foreign problems that are really not any of her business.

143

General Eisenhower felt the danger in a revival of isolationism soon after his return from Europe. In June, 1945, he said, in a speech in Kansas City:

"The problems of Europe and the world are our problems, whether we like it or not. This [the Middle West] has been called the heart of isolationism. I don't believe it. No intelligent person can be isolationist, and the ratio of intelligence here is high. If there are a few who believe we can isolate ourselves, they had better face the facts—rockets, robots swarming through the air at great speed and great distance.

"If another war should come, even in only five or ten years, no one can say these can't reach us, no matter from what distance launched."

On June 23 he spoke to his own people in Abilene along the same lines:

"No longer are we here independent of the rest of the world.

"We must sell our wheat and we must get things from the rest of the world. Our part is most important. There is nothing so important to the world today as food in a material way. Food is necessary all over Europe and must be sent to preserve the peace. In that way you see immediately your connection with the problems of Europe.

"We are not isolationists. . . . We are part of the great civilization of this world at this moment, and every part of the world where a similar civilization prevails is part of us."

In July, 1946, in an address at Amherst College before the American Alumni Council, after being presented with the Council's Award of Merit, he said:

"There was a time when an American could be, and generally was, utterly unconcerned with the outer world because the oceans set us safely apart from all other peoples. Those days are gone. Vast spaces of the earth once measured in months of travel have been reduced to daily schedules of

144

hours and minutes. Every nation is neighbor to all mankind. The need for international teamwork is no less than for that among ourselves.

"Especially important it is to realize that there can be no assured peace and tranquillity for any one nation except as it is achieved for all. So long as want, frustration, and a sense of injustice prevail among significant sections of earth, no other section can be wholly released from fear. The more terrifying become weapons of concentrated destructive power the more applicable is this truth. The glowing future of peace, confidence, and freedom that we visualize for every individual within our borders will not be completely attained until other nations can, in some degree, achieve comparable goals."

In the fall of that year, he spoke at Lafayette College after receiving an honorary degree. He went back in his illustration to show how the ignoring of international duties and ties had brought about a military weakness that took us two years to overcome in the last war and might prove fatal in the next war. After citing a warning in 1919 against isolationism and disarmament, made by General Peyton C. March, former Chief of Staff (and a Lafayette alumnus), which was ignored, he said:

"As leader within the community of nations on whose strength and guidance countless millions depend, the United States must not shirk its responsibilities, however onerous they may be. To falter in the course we have chosen, or to isolate ourselves once again, will be the prelude to another world conflict. No other sequel is possible should the United States, the earth's most powerful force for peace, abandon its present position. Into the vacuum will rush the same evil elements which nullified democracy's triumph in the first world war.

"General March's warning twenty-seven years ago is far more urgent today. Our geographical immunity has totally disappeared. Our responsibilities have multiplied. Both selfish interests and the world's future press us to a firm resolve that we shall never again through our apathy or weakness permit aggression another chance."

In a hearing before the House Committee on Foreign Affairs on the Inter-American Military Cooperation Act, in June, 1947, Eisenhower pointed out in his formal statement:

"The average American surely realizes that in event of a conflagration, the initial step would include an effort against the industrial areas of North America in the vicinity of the Great Lakes and St. Lawrence River Valley. Likewise the average citizen appreciates that these movements may be made through the air."

He told the Boy Scouts at Valley Forge in July, 1950:

"In the world conflict, national neutrality is futile, if not impossible. Therefore, we must support those with whom our kinship and our friendship are clearly established by common devotion to the freedom of men. The cost of effective help is great and the risks are sometimes fearful. But the alternative is an enslaved world. Even in the mighty United States—if surrounded solely by hostile areas, men could not permanently continue free."

On February 1, 1951, before an informal joint session of the House and Senate on his return from an inspection trip to Western Europe, Eisenhower said:

". . . standing alone and isolated in a world otherwise completely dominated by communism, our system would have to wither away. We would suffer economic atrophy and then finally collapse."

THE UNITED NATIONS

General Eisenhower, as has been evident, is convinced that nations can and must get along together, cooperating for their own sake and for the future peace. In addition to speaking of it often in general terms, he has specifically voiced his hope in the United Nations and his conviction that it *must* be made to succeed.

In his address at the State Fair at Lincoln, Nebraska, in

September, 1946, he linked the United Nations to the quality of neighborliness that is such a characteristic of the Middle West:

"The increase of the quality of neighborliness among the nations is as essential to national security as is an adequate military establishment. The social and the military aspects of security are mutually complementary.

"Mutual understanding and tolerance will build up a moral force that one day will be strong enough to make all nations secure.

"There are many ways of describing the role which we hope the United Nations will play in world politics, but I believe the very nub of its mission is the promotion of neighborly virtues among all nations, great and small.

"The task, then is not merely to get others to understand us —we have a reciprocal duty with respect to them. . . ."

In his February, 1948, final report as Chief of Staff to the Secretary of the Army, in the section devoted to his views on the long-range problem of security, he took the long view on the future of the U. N.:

"Although still unproved by time or the ordeals that will come with time, the United Nations represents so fundamental and so far-reaching a reversal of traditional attitudes toward international relations that a long period of trial and error, of test and experiment, may be necessary before the concept is proved and accepted by all states without reservation.

"During this probative period, the American people should be the last to doubt eventual success and should be foremost in combatting pessimism about the United Nations' future. . . .

"We may be certain that the development of the United Nations . . . will be . . . a long and arduous process. There will be setbacks to its popular acceptance far more discouraging than the deadlocks and wrangles of the past two years. There will be threats of secession and boycott by aggrieved disputants. There may even be war between its members, threatening its dissolution. The habit of acceptance is lacking among the member nations and will come only when the United Nations is proved an effective international instrument and when time accustoms the nations to the idea that the welfare of all is most truly the welfare of each. A generation, or even a century, may pass before the nations in concert develop practical measures to banish war from international relations. But if men can learn only by experience, the next war will surely be convincing."

And in his address in the McMillin Academic Theater at Columbia University in March, 1950, he said:

"In the broader scope, the United Nations, however halting its progress may be, however much its sessions are torn by the jeers and vetoes from one sector, is a viable and working entity—substantial evidence of developing hopes and purposes, an earnest of better things to come."

THE ATOM BOMB

On the control of this most fearful of man's weapons, General Eisenhower has indicated his agreement with the American government's efforts to have the bomb outlawed—*effectively* outlawed—by international action. The American program to achieve this, generally known as the Baruch Plan, called, among other things, for the establishment of an international inspecting agency which would have free access to atomic plants in all nations in order to see that the ban on bomb manufacture and storage was not being evaded. It was presented to the United Nations in 1946 and won overwhelming support by the member nations. But Soviet Russia, using the veto power, defeated all efforts to adopt the program for inspection to make sure of enforcement.

This situation leaves the question of the use of the A-bomb in war as a grave moral problem for the peoples of the world —especially for the people of America, who possess the greatest stockpile of the bombs. Let us see what General Eisenhower thinks about it.

His attitude toward the atom and hydrogen bombs is

practical—based on whether the military advantages outweigh the moral considerations. If great strategic gains could be made, if lives of our men could be saved and the conflict shortened, then by all means go ahead and use it. But if the military advantages are minor or dubious and their outcome uncertain, and if the use would arouse an indignation among our allies that might impede their cooperation with us or arouse genuine widespread indignation at home, then it would be only good sense to refrain.

In a press conference in San Francisco in July, 1950, he indicated no objection to using the atom bomb on a strictly military target such as a vast warehouse area, but he expanded the other point of view:

"I believe that were I in the middle of this thing [whether to use the atom bomb in Korea] I would avoid using anything that our own people or other peoples might consider inhuman. It is imperative that we stand before the world as champions of decency. I wouldn't want to do anything that might antagonize public opinion in any way. . . . We're trying to stand before the world as decent, just people, not as judges who exterminate those who oppose us."

But later he said of the hydrogen bomb:

"I can't go along with those who believe we should hide the horror of the H-bomb in ignorance. I can see no good in ignorance. From the beginning of time, every invention of mankind has been capable of two uses, good and evil. It is up to the moral fiber of mankind to decide to which use an invention is put. But certainly at this time, faced as we are with a Godless opponent, I do not believe we should bury our heads in the sand."

THE ECONOMIC WEAPON AGAINST COMMUNISM

The economic ideas of Dwight Eisenhower as they apply to the United States are based, as we have seen, on his belief in the partnership of all the producing elements of society. Strife between them endangers the welfare of all; if one element profits too much at the expense of the others there is danger both of social schisms which give rise to demagogues and of the panaceas of statism which threaten the liberties of the people.

It is logical to assume that this basic philosophy colors his attitude toward the question of American economic aid to the nations the United States counts upon as allies in the struggle with Soviet totalitarianism. It may be further assumed that it also has bearing on his attitude toward economic aid and technical advice to those areas of the world that cannot be counted upon as our allies. These areas are fertile fields for Communist infiltration because of economic inequalities between the classes of society.

On this topic it is well to keep in mind Eisenhower's pragmatic approach, as he interprets the word "pragmatic," to the economic problem. He is no tyro in economics—certainly not as concerns production for military defense. As a young officer he became an expert in the subject. His fact-gathering mind has since gone much deeper into the matter. Press reports from his headquarters near Paris after he was recalled from academic life to become Supreme Allied Commander in Europe indicate that the French were astonished at his detailed knowledge of and searching questions about the economic problems of France.

It is obvious that he believes the United States should extend all the aid that is necessary and that is within its power to help the Western European nations form a defense cordon against Soviet aggression. He has made equally clear his belief that these nations should pull their own weight—that they should not depend on the United States alone to protect them but should bear their fair share of the economic and military burden. He has spent months of effort trying to build a joint defense on this basis.

His words also indicate that he approves, in principle at least, of the purpose behind the program of economic aid and advice to underprivileged nations—the Point Four program. Its purpose is to improve the low living standards of these peoples and thereby prevent their falling prey to Communist agitation. There are other potential gains, but from the immediate standpoint of defense this is the chief one.

But if General Eisenhower goes along with the practical defensive aspects of this plan, it is by no means clear how far he thinks it should be carried. His public statements do not throw much light on this question. Quite naturally, he has not indicated how much American money he thinks should be spent to bolster the economies, for example, of India or Indonesia. But from his general outlook one may guess that he would try to judge the matter on the basis of expected practical results. For all his optimism, he is not a follower of the Henry Wallace school of economic idealism.

On the need to help destitute people he once said: "Generosity has never impoverished the giver; it has enriched the lives of those who have practiced it."

But he also has said in another connection: "By no means do I believe that the wealthy of this world can solve this great problem of disparity merely by sharing what they now possess with the less fortunate."

The development of his ideas on this subject, from the time when American aid under the United Nations Relief and Rehabilitation Administration was needed for desperate people in Europe down to the present time, is shown in these quotations.

At a hearing on November 22, 1945, before the House Foreign Affairs Committee on a bill to appropriate over a billion dollars for the purpose of UNRRA, he spoke urgently on behalf of the bill:

"World War II has left most of Europe prostrate. Many cities have been devastated beyond imagination and are a shambles of roofless walls and rubble. . . .

". . . There are few places in Europe today where people are not cold, hungry and apprehensive of the future. . . .

"I am fully confident that the people of Europe can recover from the grievous blows they have suffered if they can be helped through this period. However, if this bitter situation is not to become so disastrous as to make men wonder if it was worth while to have taken up arms against the Nazis, we in the United States—which is truly the land of plenty as compared to Europe—must be prepared to discharge a very heavy responsibility. We must, now, make our proportionate contribution to the relief of Europe in order to insure the permanence of our military victory."

In his talk before the Bureau of Advertising of the American Newspaper Publishers' Association in April, 1946, he spoke again of economic help for distressed nations:

"Our own conception of democracy, no matter how earnestly venerated by ourselves, is of little importance to men whose immediate concern is the preservation of physical life. With famine and starvation the lot of half the world, food is of far more current importance to them than are political ideas. The degree of our sacrifice in feeding the hungry is the degree of our understanding of the world today. And by our conduct toward the hungry now, our country and its institutions will not only be judged tomorrow, but our own progress toward a peaceful world will be measured."

In addition to economic aid he sees the need for greater mutual understanding as essential to world peace. "My theory is that we can all live peacefully together if we will each have a little sense, but truth is the important thing to help us develop some sense, all of us," he told a special subcommittee of the House Committee on Foreign Affairs in a hearing on a bill to set up a United States information service abroad, in February, 1947. Later, during the questioning, he said:

"As I see it, if you go into this thing you must go into it on a basis of a long-term proposition. As I say, it is not merely beaming out of facts. I would encourage the exchange of students, of scientists, of doctors, of instructors, of even theologians; anything you think of that would tend to carry back into these various countries an understanding of what we are doing and just how we live, and we, in turn, getting some clearer idea of why people act thus and so. . . . Because the more you understand these difficulties, the better will be our own programs in turn. I believe it should go in the fields of art, science, and everything. Everything educational.

"We are going to use our power, our influence and our

wealth to lift people up and to give them a chance to live their own lives. If we are to do that they must know the facts about the country on which they are depending."

Yet the United States should not and cannot indefinitely support and sustain the whole world, and that should not be expected either by others or by ourselves. In an address at Vicksburg on July 4, 1947, he said: "We are still extending ourselves to feed, clothe and minister to the wants of many peoples. This can be emergency action only—no country can permanently carry others on its back. Millions are still in want, and will not reach full sufficiency until they are able, with such help as can be given, to solve their own great problems. Basic to that solution is their freedom from fear of domination."

This thought—that we must help other nations but that they must help themselves—was repeated in his address to an informal joint session of Congress on February 1, 1951, when he spoke of conditions in Western Europe and their contributions, and ours, toward mutual defense:

"I cannot conceive that the United States ever consented to accept the responsibility for the command of Western Europe except that they had the reservation that their representatives would do their utmost to see that we are all advancing together and the United States is not being made merely an Atlas to carry the load on its shoulders. . . ."

CHAPTER XVI

Western Europe—Front Line of Democracy

"The problem of Europe and the world are
our problems, whether we like it or not."

How to defend free Western civilization along the Iron
Curtain boundary was the great problem confronting General Eisenhower on his return to active duty in the Army.

Russian conquest of Western Europe, along with Communist advances in Asia, would isolate the United States in
the Western Hemisphere. This would so change the balance
of world power that the fate of this nation would virtually be
sealed. With Western Europe's factories and skills in the
hands of the Soviet dictatorship, America would no longer
have the industrial advantage to offset the Russian, satellite
and Asiatic predominance in man power. Ike Eisenhower's
job called for an evaluation of the morale of our potential
allies, of their economic ability to meet the need, and of
our own economic ability to help them.

The superb record of the British nation under the leadership of Winston Churchill during World War II, when it
stood alone for a time against what appeared to be overwhelming odds, won the respect of Eisenhower and all other
Americans. His experience with the British later during the
joint Anglo-American invasion of the continent and overthrow of the Nazi power increased his regard for British qualities.

This has laid him open to charges of being an Anglophile
in certain political and press circles that have made a profession of hating the British. He has not denied the accusation;
he knows the nature of the British; he knows that they are the
first and foremost among the allies of the free world upon
which America can depend; he knows that Anglo-American

cooperation is the foundation of the fortress that must be built to protect our values against totalitarian attack.

He expressed his attitude toward the British in these words at the Joint Session of Congress in June, 1945:

"It was no small test of the hospitality and generous understanding of the British people to have two million strangers moved among their already limited and crowded facilities. The added confusion imposed by the extensive gear of a great army was accepted with a cheerfulness that won the admiration of us Americans.

"In critical moments Mr. Churchill did not hesitate to cut England's already reduced rations to provide more shipping for war purposes. Their overburdened railways had to absorb additional loads until practically all passenger traffic was suspended and even essential goods could be moved only on an emergency basis. For the hospitality the British offered us, for the discomforts they endured on our behalf, and for the sacrifices they made for the success of operations, every American acquainted with the facts will always carry for them a warm and grateful place deep within his heart.

"Under these two great war leaders [Roosevelt and Churchill] were the combined British-American Chiefs of Staff who were my direct military superiors and the channel through whom I received all my orders. Their unwavering support, their expressed and implied confidence, their wise direction, and their friendliness in contact, were things to which I am happy to bear witness. They devised the machinery by which huge Allied forces were put together as a single unit, and through them were implemented the great military purposes that America and Great Britain agreed upon to further the political objectives of the war."

So much for British partnership in World War II. What of the British—and the Western European peoples'—partnership with the United States in the defense cordon that is being built, nearly seven years after World War II, against a rapacious Soviet imperialism?

One of the great problems that Eisenhower has confronted in his job as head of the N.A.T.O. is whether the British are ready under the force of circumstances to change their traditional and insular balance-of-power policy toward continental Europe and enter fully into economic as well as military partnership with France and the other countries of Western Europe, including Western Germany. Winston Churchill was a sponsor of Western European cooperation to guard the ancient values of Western European civilization from the Russian threat. But how far his government will go to aid this cause is a question that is as yet unanswered.

Another and even more crucial question which General Eisenhower was called upon to evaluate when he was sent to Europe was that of the morale of the peoples. Did the nations of Western Europe, weakened if not bled white by two of history's most destructive wars and now subjected to a constant barrage of Communist propaganda, have the stamina and will to endure the additional sacrifices of rearmament and to fight, if need be, for their democratic heritage?

On the economic side of the problem, there was the question whether Western Europe's shaky economy, which had been revived by a combination of European efforts and American aid, could stand the additional strain of diverting enough of its production from butter to guns. And, back of this, was the question of how much more aid could the United States, considering its own rearmament program, furnish to Europe.

All of these things were in the mind of General Eisenhower when he returned early last year to Europe as the Supreme Allied Commander, Europe, and as the mainspring of the cooperation of the North Atlantic Treaty Organization. On his return, on January 7, 1951, he broadcast from Paris this message to the peoples of Western Europe and Britain:

"I return to Europe as a military commander, but with no miraculous plans, no display of military force. I return with an unshakable faith in Europe—this land of our ancestors—in the underlying courage of its people, in their willingness to live and sacrifice for a secure peace and the continuance and the progress of civilization.

"I approach my present task in full awareness that no

amount of outside aid alone could defend Europe. Moreover, although the North Atlantic Treaty nations have now undertaken a great cooperative enterprise for their common security, it is obvious that each must still continue the hard core of its own defense.

"In the great heritage of Europe, in the genius and productivity of its people must be found the will, the moral strength and much of the means to build defenses behind which its children may prosper and live in peace. These are the children of Europe, not just of Holland, Italy, France or other nations.

"The children of all nations deserve better than we have so far been able to promise them. They bear no hatred, suspicion or distrust. They have earned none against themselves. Let us work for them and put aside all prejudices and past grievances. And let us never shirk from defending their birthright of liberty, even as ours has been cherished and stanchly defended for us.

"I cling to the hope that the young lives, the blood and suffering of the last war, were not spent as the profligate squanders his inheritance—but that from the common ordeal will now rise up a strong and united Europe, a Europe that can look forward confidently to a future of peace, advancement and mutual security.

"This is our goal. We must put our hearts and hands to its achievement.

"No lesser purpose, no warped nationalism, and above all, no aggressive or predatory design, should be allowed to turn us away from this noble enterprise. In the same degree that we believe danger threatens us all, we must meet it together. Our task is to preserve the peace, not to incite war. We approach that task not in appeasement, but with the clear eyes and stout hearts of men who know that theirs is a righteous cause.

"There is power in our union—and resoucefulness on sea, land and air. Aroused and united, there is nothing which the nations of the Atlantic community cannot achieve.

"Let those who might be tempted to put this power to the test ponder well the lessons of history. The cause of freedom can never be defeated.

"We are committed to a great partnership and I, in all humility, am proud to serve in one phase of attaining the aspirations of our several peoples. Should mankind, through our solidarity, our prayers for peace, and through the mercy of God, be spared the catastrophe of another war, then this organization will have served a noble purpose.

"It will have demonstrated that an alliance for peace rather than for war is an entirely practical matter—that the power generated in an alliance of such magnitude can bring confidence—not fear—to the hearts of men."

After a tour of inspection of the Western European countries in which he sounded out the leaders of the various nations on what each country could contribute to the common defense and formed his own ideas of European morale, he returned to report to the Congress and the American people. Then he went back to his crucial job in Europe. His conclusions were set forth in two speeches, one his report to Congress on February 1, 1951, and the other a broadcast to the American people on February 2, 1951. The speeches are not altogether repetitive, but excerpts from the broadcast serve to convey the General's message. In it he set forth the necessity for combined defense and the terrible alternative for the United States if the effort were not made:

"Our hope remains the achievement of peace based on understanding and forbearance, the only sure foundation for peace.

"We must never lose faith that such a peace can be ultimately established. We seek such a peace and no one can honestly interpret our current modest preparations otherwise.

"But we should examine the current situation fearlessly and clearly, neither shutting our eyes to obvious dangers nor permitting fear to warp our judgment. America's record and America's strength certainly should prevent hysterical apprehension of the future.

"Today, we are faced by an aggressive imperialism that has more than once announced its implacable hostility to free government. Therefore, we strive to erect a wall of security for the free world behind which free institutions can live. That wall must be maintained until Communist imperialism dies of its own inherent evils.

"One of the great questions before us is the will and capacity of Europe to cooperate effectively in this aim. Unless there exists in Europe a will to defend itself, no amount of outside help can possibly make it secure. A nation's defense must spring from its own soul; and the soul cannot be imported.

"For years, we have heard that Western Europe is plagued, confused, and divided far more seriously than we are; we have heard that in their homes, in factories, on the street, millions of honest workmen are daily subjected to Communist bullying, that their days and nights are haunted by the specter of invading hordes whom they cannot hope to equal in numbers or physical strength.

"Furthermore, the discouragement, destruction, and confusion visited upon the peoples of Europe by two World Wars sapped their productive capacity and, in some instances, reduced them to levels of near starvation. More than this—their spirit was smothered in war-weariness.

"That is a story often told. If it were the whole story, then all I could honestly do would be to recommend that we abandon the N.A.T.O. treaty and—by ourselves—attempt, however, futilely, to build a separate fortress against threatening aggression. Two striking facts make such a recommendation, for me, impossible.

"The first fact is that the utter hopelessness of the alternative requires our participation in European defense. We can all understand that America must be strong in air and sea power. These elements are vitally essential to the defense of the free world and it is through them that we protect the approaches to our homeland and the routes of commerce necessary to our existence.

"But this alone is not enough. Our ships will not long sail the seas, nor our planes fly the world airways, if we stand aside in fancied security while an aggressive imperialism sweeps over areas of the earth with which our own future is inseparably linked.

"Western Europe is the cradle of our civilization; from her originally we drew our strength, genius, and culture. But our concern in Europe is far more than sentimental. Our own security is directly involved. Europe is a highly developed industrial complex with the largest and most varied pool of skilled labor on earth. This huge potential would be a rich prize for a totalitarian invasion. Its direct importance to us is the stark fact that its possession by Communist forces would give them opportunity to develop a preponderance of power. Even this disaster would not tell the whole story.

"If Western Europe should be overrun by communism, many economically dependent areas in Africa and the Middle East would be affected by the debacle. Southeastern Asia would probably soon be lost. Thus, we would be cut off from the raw materials of all these regions—materials that we need for existence. World destiny would then be dictated by imperialistic powers whose avowed purpose is the destruction of freedom.

"The second fact bearing upon our participation in European defense is that the people of Europe are not spiritually bankrupt, despite the validity of many pessimistic reports. Great sections of its population have for years labored on and fought the creeping paralysis of communism. Now, the North Atlantic Treaty has brought new fuel to the flames of hope in Europe. It has noticeably lifted morale, the fundamental element in this whole situation—the force which powers all human progress.

"In every capital, there is growing a desire to cooperate in this mutual security effort. All the Governments that I have recently visited agreed that their defense programs must be stepped up despite economic and other difficulties—in spite of preoccupations that constitute abnormal drains upon particular nations.

.   .   .   .

"In every country, I saw heartening evidence of a regeneration in Europe's spirit. Its morale, its will to fight, will grow with every accretion to physical strength. The arrival in Europe of new American land and air units, though modest in protective influence by themselves, will certainly produce added confidence and accelerate the production of military force throughout the member nations.

"The European nations must, of course, produce and maintain the great bulk of the land forces necessary to their defense.

"For this purpose, the most immediate need of Europe is munitions and equipment. Every one of the continental nations I visited can rapidly and markedly increase its resistance power if it can be promptly furnished additional supplies of this kind. To fill this need, our loyal neighbor, Canada, with Britain and others, is shouldering part of the load.

"In military potential, the free nations have everything they need—natural resources, industrial genius, productive capacity, and great reservoirs of leadership ability. Given the ingredient of morale—the determination to combine for mutual protection—the military strength necessary will be produced at a speedy pace. With every increase in strength, there will be an upward thrust in morale, resulting in an ever-mounting spiral of confidence and security.

"With respect to time, no man can know at what hour, if ever, our defensive organization may be put to the ultimate test. Because our purpose is entirely defensive, we must be ready at the earliest possible moment. Only an aggressor could name the day and hour of attack. Our current mobilization, properly adjusted to our peaceful security needs, should be as rapid as any required by the emergency of war.

"To you, the people of America, I repeat—as I have to the Congress and to the President—that I believe,

"First, the preservation of free America requires our participation in the defense of Western Europe.

"Second, success is attainable. Given unity in spirit and action, the job can be done.

"Third, while the transfer to Europe of American military units is essential, our major and special contribution should be in the field of munitions and equipment.

"By no means, do I believe that we Americans can support the world militarily or economically. In our own interest, we must insist upon a working partnership with every nation making the common security its task of first priority. Every one of the member nations must realize that the success of this combined effort to preserve the peace rests as directly upon America's productive, economic, and political strength as it does on any amount of military force we can develop. Only cooperative effort by all of us can preserve for the free world a position of security, relative peace, and economic stability.

"Attainment of this result is largely a matter of morale and the human spirit. The free world now must prove itself worthy of its own past.

"If Frenchmen can rise to the heights their fathers achieved at Verdun in 1916; if Italians can recapture the fervor of Vittorio Veneto; if the British can relive the days of 1940 when they stood alone against Hitler; if our other Allies can react to today's threat in the mode of their own revered patriots; if we, here in America, can match the courage and self-sacrifice of the ragged, freezing members of Washington's Army at Valley Forge; indeed, if each of us now proves himself worthy of his countrymen fighting and dying in Korea, then success is sure—a glorious success that will bring us security, confidence, tranquillity.

"Each of us must do his part. We cannot delay, nationally or individually, while we suspiciously scrutinize the sacrifices made by our neighbor, and, through a weasling logic, seek some way to avoid our own duties.

"If we Americans seize the lead, we will preserve and be worthy of our own past. Our children will dwell in peace. They will dwell in freedom. They will read the history of this decade with tingling pride and, from their kinship with this generation, they will inherit more than can be expressed in millions, in acres, or in world acclaim."

CHAPTER XVII

A United States of Europe

"A nation's success in war and peace demands participation in the community of nations."

Brought up with a sense of the practical value of cooperation and community effort, Eisenhower learned from his study of American history the benefits that derived from the hard-won union of the thirteen small and weak American states. Like many Americans, he has felt that this was a precedent that could be applied to the solution of Europe's age-old struggle for national hegemony.

He was not naive or lacking in appreciation of the difficulties involved. He knew the ancient quarrels and local prejudices that separated these people—people of a common West European culture. But his optimism and his spirit of practicality indicated to him, as it had to some of the more farsighted leaders of the Western European nations, that economic and perhaps even political union were the only answers to the problem of survival.

He voiced this hope at an address in Philadelphia in May, 1948. Three years later he repeated the idea briefly before a subcommittee of the Senate Foreign Relations Committee, on July 9, 1951:

"Personally I am very hopeful that many of our problems would disappear if this whole area of Western Europe were one federal union. I believe it so strongly that I do not believe real security is going to be felt in the United States, in the British Empire, and other nations of the globe until that comes about. I just don't believe it. We can approach it slowly, and probably obtain a great measure of success;

enough, at least, to establish an uneasy truce. But I believe the day this whole area in Western Europe gets united—and once it gets united—the Soviets will never be able to hold the East Germans out of it—I believe that with all my heart."

Six days before that he had spoken his views on European unity in an address before the English-Speaking Union in London. Winston Churchill, himself a judge of oratory, is said to have considered this one of the great speeches of the twentieth century. Excerpts are given below:

"One hundred seventy-five years ago, the founding fathers of the American Republic declared their independence of the British Crown. Little could they have known—in the heat and bitterness of the hour—that the severance, accomplished in passion, would through the years flower into an alliance of such fitness and worth that it was never recorded on legal parchment, but in the hearts of our two peoples. The bond that joins us—stronger than blood lines, than common tongue and common law—is the fundamental conviction that man was created to be free, that he can be trusted with freedom, that governments have as a primary function the protection of his freedom.

.   .   .   .

"In that spirit our countries are joined with the peoples of Western Europe and the North Atlantic to defend the freedoms of western civilization. Opposed to us—cold and forbidding—is an ideological front that marshals every weapon in the arsenal of dictatorship. Subversion, propaganda, deceit and the threat of naked force are daily hurled against us and our friends in a globe-encircling, relentless campaign.

.   .   .   .

"The stand in Korea should serve notice in this area as well as in the Far East, that we will resist aggression with all the force at our command. Our effort to provide security against the possibility of another and even greater emergency—an emergency which will never be of our making—must go forward with the same resolution and courage that has characterized our Korean forces. The member nations in the North Atlantic Treaty Organization need not fear the future or any Communistic threat if we are alert, realistic and resolute. Our community possesses a potential might that far surpasses the sinister forces of slave camp and chained millions. But to achieve the serenity and the confidence that our potential can provide, we must press forward with the mobilization of our spiritual and intellectual strength; we must develop promptly the material force that will assure the safety of our friends upon the continent and the security of the free world.

"This is the challenge of our times that, until satisfactorily met, establishes priorities in all our thoughts, our work, our sacrifices. The hand of the aggressor is stayed by strength—and strength alone!

"Although the security of each of us is bound up in the safety of all of us, the immediate threat is most keenly felt by our partners in Europe. Half of the continent is already within the monolithic mass of totalitarianism. The drawn and haunted faces in the docks of the purge courts are grim evidence of what Communistic domination means. It is clearly necessary that we quickly develop maximum strength within free Europe itself. Our own interests demand it.

"It is a truism that where, among partners, strength is demanded in its fullness, unity is the first requisite. Without unity, the effort becomes less powerful in application, less decisive in result. This fact has special application in Europe. It would be difficult indeed to overstate the benefits, in these years of stress and tension, that would accrue to N.A.T.O. if the free nations of Europe were truly a unit.

"But in that vital region, history, custom, language and prejudice have combined to hamper integration. Progress has been and is hobbled by a web of customs barriers interlaced with bilateral agreements, multilateral cartels, local shortages, and economic monstrosities. How tragic! Free men, facing the specter of political bondage, are crippled by artificial bonds that they themselves have forged, and they alone can loosen! Here is a task to challenge the efforts of the wisest statesmen, the best economists, the most brilliant diplomats.

"European leaders, seeking a sound and wise solution, are spurred by the vision of a man at this table—a man of inspiring courage in dark hours, of wise counsel in grave decisions. Winston Churchill's plea for a united Europe can yet bear such greatness of fruit that it may well be remembered as the most notable achievement of a career marked by achievement.

"The difficulties of integrating Western Europe of course appear staggering to those who live by ritual. But great majorities in Europe earnestly want liberty, peace and the opportunity to pass on to their children the fair lands and the culture of Western Europe. They deserve, at the very least, a fair chance to work together for the common purpose; freed of the costly encumbrances they are now compelled to carry.

"Europe cannot attain the towering material stature possible to its peoples' skills and spirit so long as it is divided by patchwork territorial fences. They foster localized instead of common interest. They pyramid every cost with middle-men, tariffs, taxes, and overheads. Barred, absolutely, are the efficient division of labor and resources and the easy flow of trade. In the political field, these barriers promote distrust and suspicion. They serve vested interests at the expense of peoples and prevent truly concerted action for Europe's own and obvious good.

"This is not to say that, as a Commander, I have found anything but ready cooperation among the Governments of Western Europe. Time and again, I have saluted from my heart the spirit of their armed services—of officers and men alike—from the mountains of Italy to the fjords of Norway, from Normandy to the Curtain. Within political circles, I have found statesmen eager to assure the success of their current defense programs. I have no doubts as to the capacity of N.A.T.O. to surmount even the formidable obstacles imposed upon us by the political facts of present-day Europe. Yet with the handicaps of enforced division, it is clear that even the minimum essential security effort will seriously strain the resources of Europe. We ignore this danger at our peril since the effects of economic failure would be disastrous upon spiritual and material strength alike. True security never rests upon the shoulders of men denied a decent present and the hope of a better future.

"But with unity achieved, Europe could build adequate

166

security and, at the same time, continue the march of human betterment that has characterized western civilization. Once united, the farms and factories of France and Belgium, the foundries of Germany, the rich farmlands of Holland and Denmark, the skilled labor of Italy, will produce miracles for the common good. In such unity is a secure future for these peoples. It would mean early independence of aid from America and other Atlantic countries. The coffers, mines and factories of that continent are not inexhaustible. Dependence upon them must be minimized by the maximum in cooperative effort. The establishment of a workable European federation would go far to create confidence among people everywhere that Europe was doing its full and vital share in giving this cooperation.

"Any soldier contemplating this problem would be moved to express an opinion that it cannot be attacked successfully by slow infiltration, but only by direct and decisive assault, with all available means.

.   .   .   .

"The winning of freedom is not to be compared to the winning of a game—with the victory recorded forever in history. Freedom has its life in the heart, the actions, the spirit of men and so it must be daily earned and refreshed—else like a flower cut from its life-giving roots, it will wither and die.

"All of us have pledged our word, one to the other, that this shall not be. We have cut the pattern for our effort—we are devoting to it available resources for its realization. We fight not only our own battle—we are defending for all mankind those things that allow personal dignity to the least of us—those things that permit each to believe himself important in the eyes of God. We are preserving opportunity for men to lift up their hearts and minds to the highest places—there must be no stragglers in such a conflict.

"The road ahead may be long—it is certain to be marked by critical and difficult passages. But if we march together, endure together, share together, we shall succeed—we shall *gloriously* succeed together!"

CHAPTER XVIII

World Peace—A Balance Sheet

"We must not be discouraged by the inescapable slowness of world progress."

As Dwight Eisenhower's stature grew, his horizons steadily broadened. As he progressed from normal boyhood to the minor responsibilities of a junior army officer, then to the immense responsibilities of the Supreme Commander of the Allied Armies in Western Europe, and finally to the position of one of the greatest and most popular figures in American history, he developed an ever-deepening wisdom and an ever more far-reaching outlook on the problems of humanity.

In this book his views on many questions, domestic and foreign, have been outlined. There remains a final summing up in his own words of the practical philosophy which is his great contribution toward answering the needs of his fellow Americans and the troubled peoples of other lands in this century of change, and of great upheavals.

This summing up was given in one of his most important, though not one of the most recent, of his addresses. It sets forth more completely his thoughts on America's role in the world and on international relationships and world peace, than any other of his many utterances. The title was "World Peace—A Balance Sheet." In it he stated his view of what must be done to insure the peaceful future progress of the United States and all other well-meaning peoples. It was delivered at the McMillin Academic Theater at Columbia University on March 23, 1950. Much of the speech is included in the following extracts:

"In discussing war and peace, we incline to paint one all black and the other all white. We like to repeat, 'There never was a good war or a bad peace.' But war often has provided the setting for comradeship and understanding and greatness of spirit—among nations as well as men—beyond anything in quiet days; while peace may be marked by, or may even be the product of, chicanery, treachery, and the temporary triumph of expediency over all spiritual values.

"The pact of Munich was a more fell blow to humanity than the atomic bomb at Hiroshima. Suffocation of human freedom among a once free people, however quietly and peacefully accomplished, is more far-reaching in its implications and its effects on their future than the destruction of their homes, industrial centers and transportation facilities. Out of rubble heaps, willing hands can rebuild a better city; but out of freedom lost can stem only generations of hate and bitter struggle and brutal oppression.

"Nor can we forget that, as Professor Lyman Bryson of Teachers College recently said: 'There are even greater things in the world than peace.' By greater things, he meant the ideals, the hopes and aspirations of humanity; those things of the soul and spirit which great men of history have valued far above peace and material wealth and even life itself.

"Without these values, peace is an inhuman existence. Far better risk a war of possible annihilation than grasp a peace which would be the certain extinction of free man's ideas and ideals.

. . . . . .

"Because there is one towering force in the world that often seems bent upon engulfing as much territory and as many people as it can, a great many surrender their hopes for peace as curtly as they write off our friends in Western Europe. Such pessimism invites disaster. Such an attitude, if it were founded on reason, would mean that the handful of men who dictate the policy of the Soviet system also dictate the fate of this globe. To anyone ready to study the history of yesterday and the facts of today, that is a repugnant absurdity.

"Granted that at any moment some one powerful nation could choose to follow a policy of world conquest by war. Nevertheless, the world has seen so many examples of this that, today, such a war would imply either an incredible stupidity, weakness, disunity and unreadiness on one side or a miscalculation equal to that of insanity and moral guilt on the side of the predatory nation. Until war is eliminated from international relations, unpreparedness for it is well nigh as criminal as war itself.

"What then is the nature of the peace that we seek? What are the characteristics that distinguish it? These questions must be answered if we are to know our objective, calculate our distance from it, decide on the measures necessary to its attainment.

"Almost certainly, most men would agree that peace, to merit the name, should possess a reasonable assurance of permanence, should be the product of cooperation between all major nations, and should be secure against arbitrary violation by any power or group of powers. It is apparent, however, that we constantly use the word *'peace'* in two senses which differ sharply. One is the peace of our dreams—a peace founded in noble impulses, universally shared. It is always the ideal, the pole star that guides us on the proper path. The other peace is *something* of an armed truce; but today a half-loaf is better than none. By the improvisations, expediencies and agreements under which we strive to maintain a peace based as much upon force and power as upon concepts of justice and fair play, we hope to reach the point where this peace becomes the starting point of the *real* peace we seek.

"But permanence, universality and security cannot be achieved *merely* by covenant or agreement. Treaties are too often scraps of paper; in our age the signal for two World Wars was the callous repudiation of pacts and pledged word. There must be a universal urge to decency.

"This fact compels the observation that they are thinking wishfully who pin their hopes of peace upon a single 'high level' conference and a resulting paper that would bear the promise of governmental heads to observe all the rights of others. An agreement, though it should bear the seal and ribbon of every chancellery in the world, is worth no more than the seal and ribbon of each signer in the good faith and integrity of every other. We must sadly acknowledge that today such world-wide confidence does not exist.

"By all means let us continue to confer—especially with

the view and purpose of reaching the required level of mutual faith and confidence, or—as a substitute—of developing practical and mutually enforceable measures and reciprocal arrangements calculated to lessen the danger of war. But, equally, let us not delude ourselves that, in 1950, establishment of real peace is merely a matter of Very Important Personages signing papers or 'talking tough' in Paris, Geneva, Washington or Tahiti.

"It is obvious that an enduring world-wide and secure peace must be founded on justice, opportunity and freedom for all men of good will; be maintained in a climate of international understanding and cooperation; be free from militaristic menace; and be supported by an accepted and respected police power representing all nations. Critical factors in the problem of building such a peace are the needs of a human society, comprised of individuals; and, further, the needs of a human society that is divided into independent nations, each sovereign within its own borders and competing with all others to promote the interests of its own citizens, often at the expense of others. There are two sides to the coin of peace, the individual and the national; if one is defective the coin is spurious.

"On the side of the individual, peace requires an international society that is free from vicious provocations to strife among men. These are rooted in inequities so glaring that, to those who suffer them, they seem to make attractive any alternative. The gamble of war lures the desperate, for even overwhelming defeat can hardly worsen their state; while victory, if it gives the survivors any improvement, will be worth its cost in blood. It is possible, even probable, that hopelessness among a people can be a far more potent cause of war than greed. War—in such case—is a symptom, not the disease.

"On the collective side of the coin, peace requires an international society liberated from the threat of aggression by neighbor on neighbor, a threat forever present when one or more nations are committed to the building or maintenance of gigantic military machines. No sane man will challenge, under present circumstances, the need for defensive strength designed to secure against internal or external attack the independence and sovereignty of a free state. But the continued existence of even one purely offensive force—a force for which there is no apparent need based in the logic of self-defense—denies enduring peace to the world. Those who have spawned such a force must either eventually destroy it by demobilization and find justification for the heavy cost already laid on their people; or use it, tacitly or actively, as a threat or as a weapon. There is no middle course.

"Always it has been difficult to distinguish between offensive and defensive armaments. Advancing science has obliterated whatever qualitative differences that once existed; today even the atom bomb is included in defensive arsenals. But differences do exist—vital differences. They are found, partially, in the quantitative factor.

"The world forms its own sound opinion of a nation's martial purposes, primarily by the size and combinations of armaments supported, and by their geographical disposition and estimated state of readiness. To be considered also is the record of the particular nation—the extent to which it observes the ordinary rules of decency, courtesy, fairness and frankness in dealing with others.

.   .   .   .   .   .

"I might state here also that the Baruch Plan for the control of the atomic bomb was not only evidence of our peaceful intent, but was the most generous action ever made by any nation, equivalent in its field to the Marshall Plan.

"Moreover, without American leadership in the search, the pursuit of a just and enduring peace is hopeless. Nowhere in the world—outside this land—is there the richness of resources, stamina and will needed to lead what at times may be a costly and exhausting effort. *But* leadership cannot be exercised by the weak. It demands strength—the strength of this great nation when its people are united in purpose, united in a common fundamental faith, united in their readiness to work for human freedom and peace; this spiritual and economic strength in turn, must be reinforced in a still armed world by the physical strength necessary for the defense of ourselves and our friends.

.   .   .   .   .

"Our twentieth century international record, the statistics of our military forces, and the open procedures of our political system—all provide proof of our peaceful purposes; they prove also that our support of programs, in which universal peace will be secure, is as honest as it is sturdy.

"The two requisites to an enduring peace—the elimination of deep-seated incitements to strife and hopelessness, and the elimination of armament for aggression—are, or should be, within the realm of feasible attainment. But man can remake the face of his physical environment and can harness all the powers of the universe more easily, it seems, than he can learn control of his temper as a member of the international community. Nevertheless, those who term these twin requisites utopian and visionary are cut from the same bolt of cloth as those of an earlier day who claimed that epidemics were an inescapable companion to human existence and denounced the preachers of sanitation as balkers of God's will.

"To prevent the crime of war, all nations and all ideologies can unite without sacrifice of principle. But lest self-interest in minor matters breed a carelessness toward the gravity of this problem, there is required unity of understanding concerning the facts of modern war. After the world-wide devastation that grows daily more possible, none may be able to distinguish between the victor and the vanquished of a future conflict. Confronted by that outcome to another World War, all of us—East and West—are in the same boat. The boat can be swamped in a series of atomic blasts; but, sustained by understanding of a common peril, it can also carry us through to final peace. Thus, the possibility of total destruction, terrible though it is, could be a blessing as all nations, great and small, for the first time in human history, are confronted by an inescapable physical proof of their common lot. Franklin's 'If we don't all hang together, we shall each hang separately' has its international application today. There is no prod so effective as a common dread; there is no binder so unifying.

. . . .

"By every step that the nations take toward more productive and efficient use of land, toward better production and distribution of food, toward raising the living standards of

173

even the least of the world's tribes; by every schoolhouse that is built where none was before; by every plague spot that is cleansed and made healthful; by every increase in the sum of universally shared knowledge and the consequent increase in each man's mastery of his environment; by every measure that enlarges men's opportunity to develop all their talents and capacities—by that much we reduce the stockpile of grievance, injustice and discontent on which war feeds.

"You say in objection: 'Those are fine words, but all history proves that as man has advanced in material and intellectual strength, wars have not lessened in frequency but have grown in the tragedy and terror of their impact.'

"To that objection I retort: The unrest that has tripped the world is, at least partially, due to the failure of the more fortunate to realize that their own self-interest requires them to teach others the techniques of raising human standards of existence. Thus, ostentatious wealth in fortunate areas has occasioned bitterness and envy in other localities where these could have been eliminated at no greater cost than that involved in teaching man to make the best use of the material resources surrounding him.

"By no means do I believe that the wealthy of this world can solve this great problem of disparity merely by sharing what they now possess with the less fortunate. What is needed is the knowledge and understanding—the technical progress—that will allow all men to make the best use of nature's bounty. Progress in this direction is already an announced American purpose. Past failures to do more in this line have provided the demagogues and the propagandists of history with much of the ammunition they have used; and the war-maker is first of all a propagandist.

"The nations now have the technical knowledge and skill to end some flagrant disparities. The same measures that banished the scourge of cholera or of typhus or malaria from the American city can largely banish all pestilence from all the continents of the earth. The machines that have released the peoples of the West from the age-old drudgeries of a hand-to-mouth existence can liberate the peoples of all lands whose bitter bread is earned in exhausted bodies and shortened lives. And, certainly, there is no need for starvation at any spot in a world that is glutted in so many places with crops, great beyond domestic needs, that must rot or be destroyed.

"Here again we must not be discouraged by the inescapable slowness of world progress. However disappointing may be the lack of speed, every new evidence of advance brings immediate hope of a brighter morrow to millions; and peoples hopeful of their domestic future do not use war as a solution to their problems. Hope spurs humans everywhere to work harder, to endure more now that the future may be better; but despair is the climate of war and death. Even America, without American optimism, can accomplish nothing beyond the needs of each day.

"Now while we attack the physical evils, we must battle the ignorance which permits them. And I mean not only ignorance in the individual human being, but those attitudes, policies and prejudices which balk the free exchange between the nations of information and knowledge that will make human living a more full expression of man's dignity. No scrap of knowledge whose only effect is to make life better should be denied any nation by any other nation. Even the Soviets, living behind a curtain woven from fear, could afford to work with the rest of us, *now,* for this decent and human objective. Though we may be generous, we can still expect rebuffs and gibes. But there is always the chance and the hope that hostile governments will understand, over the years, the honesty of our motives and join with us in their realization. If or when they do, we will all profit and we— both West and East—will sleep easier of nights.

"Another thing—the stresses and strains of fear are intensified in our day because everywhere the superstitions of materialism are increasing their holds on the minds of men. Hundreds of millions live within the Communist orbit where the official doctrine makes mankind the helpless pawn of economic forces.

"But man's spiritual side is still the dominant one. No human, whatever his position in the social hierarchy or his job in the working economy, merits more respect than any other animal of the woods or fields unless we accept without reservation the brotherhood of man under the Fatherhood of God. If men are not creatures of soul, as well as of body, they are

175

not better than the field mule, harnessed to the plow, whipped and goaded to work, cared for in the measure of his cost and value. But too often, today, we incline to describe the ultimate in human welfare as a mule's sort of heaven—a tight roof overhead, plenty of food, a minimum of work and no worries or responsibilities. So far have we strayed in our sense of values. Unless we rekindle our own understanding, can we hope to make Marxist devotees see that things of the spirit—justice, freedom, equality—are the elements that make important the satisfaction of man's creative needs? If I doubted that man is something more than mere educated animal I should personally be little concerned in the question of war or peace.

"Even under the most propitious of circumstances, the obstacles to growth of understanding are legion in number and staggering in their mass. Hundreds of millions behind the Iron Curtain are daily drilled in the slogan: 'There is no God, and religion is an opiate.' But not all the people within the Soviet accept this fallacy; and some day they will educate their rulers—or change them. True enough, too, there are many places where men of one color seem bent on degrading men of another color, shearing them of their dignity and standing as fellow-beings. But the human conscience comes gradually to recognize this injustice and men of good purpose will grasp at any reasonable solution to eliminate it.

"We cannot, of course, attain perfection in human relations even within the smallest community, no matter how many laws we pass or policemen we hire. The rogue and the villain skulk in dark corners. But as we put street lamps on these corners so that decent folk may walk abroad after dark, so we can re-light the lamps of brotherhood where they have been extinguished among men. Again we see that the fortunate will serve their own best interests by eliminating injustice and its consequent urge toward strife.

. . . . .

"There is no need to remake the world, outside the Soviet system, in the likeness of the United States or any other country. What I do suggest is that we recognize that every culture

176

developed in the world has been worked out by its possessors to meet the circumstances of their own environment. Each race and each nation can learn from every other. There is none so close to self-sufficiency that it can do without the help and cooperation of others; none so primitive that it has not amassed a wisdom that can possibly enlighten even the most advanced.

"The free world has already committed itself to attainment of our two basic conditions for permanent peace—the satisfaction of human hungers and a climate of international understanding and good will. Much has been done toward their achievement. The transformation of the world thus far accomplished is at least half a miracle. Moreover, the spokesmen of the Soviets declare that they too are dedicated to the same purpose. Parenthetically, I might add, if *their* methods succeed, it would be, to us, a complete miracle.

"Nevertheless, all governments pay an equal lip service to the common purpose of satisfying human hungers and promoting international understanding. Every one of them, if challenged, can point to laws and policies that are noble beyond criticism. Why, then, is not world peace automatically ours?

"Simply because the positive elements in the construction of peace can be nullified by any powerfully armed nation, whose motives are suspect, unless all are committed to disarmament and there is some means of enforcing peace among them. All the sanitary safeguards ever designed will not secure a community against disease if the residents of one block flaunt them; and the violators will not be persuaded to amend their ways until health officers, backed by the police and the laws, enforce the ordinances.

"When even one major power, surreptitiously or flagrantly, builds and maintains a military machine beyond the recognized needs of reasonable security, a war of aggression is a constant threat to peaceful nations. At the very least, these armaments become the gangsters' gun—a notice that might and might alone shall serve as judge and jury and sheriff in the settling of international dispute. That is the only realistic interpretation, since no government otherwise would squander its revenue or exhaust its economy on so sterile an enterprise. It is clear that international disarmament is essential to a stable, enduring peace.

"In a disarmed world—should it be attained—there must be an effective United Nations with a police power universally recognized and strong enough to earn universal respect. In it the individual nations can pool the power for policing the continents and the seas against *international* lawlessness—those acts which involve two or more nations in their *external* relations.

"I do not subscribe to any idea that a world police force or a world organization should be permitted entrance to any nation for the purpose of settling disputes among its citizens, or for exercising any authority not specifically and voluntarily accorded by the affected nation. At this stage of civilization's progress any effort to push to this extreme the purpose of international law enforcement will defeat legitimate objectives. National sovereignty and independence have been won by most at too great cost to surrender to an external agency such powers. But by the establishment of a United Nations police of properly defined and restricted but effective powers, no nation would surrender one iota of its current national functions or authority, for none, by itself, now possesses a shred of responsibility to police the world. To an international peace organization, a nation would give up nothing beyond its equitable share in men and money.

. . . .

"As friends of free people everywhere in the world, we can by our own example—our conduct in every crisis, real or counterfeit; our resistance to propaganda and passion; our readiness to seek adjustment and compromise of difference—we can by our own example ceaselessly expand understanding among the nations. We must never forget that international friendship is achieved through rumors ignored, propaganda challenged and exposed; through patient loyalty to those who have proved themselves worthy of it; through help freely given, where help is needed and merited. In this sense there is no great, no humble among us. In rights and in opportunity, in loyalty and in responsibility to ideals, we are and must remain equal. Peace is more the product of our day-to-day living than of a spectacular program, intermittently executed.

"The best foreign policy is to live our daily lives in honesty, decency and integrity; at home, making our own land a more fitting habitation for free men; and, abroad, joining with those of like mind and heart, to make of the world a place where all men can dwell in peace. Neither palsied by fear nor duped by dreams but strong in the rightness of our purpose, we can then place our case and cause before the bar of world opinion—history's final arbiter between nations."

CHAPTER XIX

The Man and the Times

The forces of history and the great strength and resources of the United States together have given to this nation a unique kind of world leadership in the postwar era. It is leadership based not on conquest or coercion but on the confidence of other peoples in America's integrity and aims—a confidence created by frankness, fair-dealing and evidence that American power is being used only to save the free world from Soviet slavery. But most Americans did not seek this pre-eminence. It was thrust upon them. And some, it seems, do not fully comprehend its nature. World leadership has brought with it perplexities and dangers that have caused confusion and doubt. In the midst of great power and responsibilities, Americans are divided and fearful of the future.

The same historic forces, plus his own character and ability, have raised Dwight David Eisenhower to a unique position of personal leadership that parallels that of his country. In Europe his magnetic personality has spurred our allies to the crucial task of building a joint defense. At home his example and the things he stands for revive hope and confidence among a troubled people. But there the parallel between nation and man ends. Unlike many of his countrymen, Eisenhower accepts the responsibilities of American leadership and its democratic goals with no division in his own mind, with no doubts and no fears of the future.

Perhaps that is why Eisenhower, amid the nation's present uncertainties and frustrations, represents to so many people the source of counsel and guidance that the democratic but somewhat impatient American mind demands when it is in trouble. He symbolizes the kind of leadership that the Republic badly needs.

But when a living man becomes a symbol there is always

the danger of substituting the reputation for the actuality, of depending on the symbol rather than the person. In Eisenhower's case, what are the differences between the symbol and the person, and how do they blend? Much of what he thinks has already been set forth in his own words. The kind of person he actually is is indicated to a considerable extent by his background, training and adult development. But, in summation, a few more facets of the reputation and certain qualities of the person may well be examined.

Consider first his qualities as a military commander. This may seem unnecessary in view of his achievements. However, there has been a tendency in some quarters to regard him as primarily a diplomatic coordinator and administrator of the war-time Allied effort rather than as one of the great strategical commanders of history. The estimates of some of the wisest military critics, as well as of the German generals he defeated, refute this idea.

He was a great and daring strategist who did not fritter away his resources in piecemeal attacks but picked the weak spot and threw all he had into it. The classic example of this was the Normandy invasion when he concentrated all his forces on the capture of the Cotentin peninsula and on the breakthrough of German defenses that followed. When the breakthrough came he quickly changed set plans and unleashed Patton's armored columns to drive across France toward the German border. The German generals considered him a great commander because, although at times he seemed to take a gambler's chance (North Africa, Italy, the French campaign), he always succeeded. He succeeded because his daring strategy was based on realistic planning.

Early in his military career he learned to discipline his mental life. He objectively measured his performances against the ideal and against what other great generals had done in like circumstance. One phase of this self-discipline was seen in his impatience with discursiveness and verbal rambling. In reports from his subordinates he demanded the point of the matter. The gist of almost any subject could and should be presented in a page.

There is the story of the time when one of his assistants, charged with preparing a report on the European and North

African campaigns for future students of history, presented a lengthy document. Eisenhower quickly glanced through it and asked the assistant what he knew about the Punic Wars. After listening to the attempted résumé, he said, in effect, that he thought so, and he pointed out that future knowledge of the European phases of World War II would be as vague unless those who took part in it prepared a brief, simple statement of what happened. The result was a nutshell history in less than a thousand words.

Another characteristic as a military commander was Eisenhower's readiness to take complete responsibility for any reverses those under him sustained. It was his view that the job of the commander-in-chief required this, regardless of whose fault it was. He knew how to delegate authority; he backed up the subordinate with everything he could give and did not interfere with the subordinate's plans; but he insisted on results.

His informal, friendly approach in dealing with people of high or low degree and his innate modesty in accepting high honors were qualities that endeared him to millions. As Anne O'Hare McCormick, of *The New York Times,* noted when he received British acclaim soon after the war: "Eisenhower is certainly the hero of Britain, but the role of hero amuses and irks him. His ingrained simplicity is untouched by adulation and he seems singularly free from either vanity or ambition."

This simplicity is indeed ingrained, and it has bearing on both Eisenhower the person and Eisenhower the symbol—if, indeed, the two can be separated. It is based on a self-confidence that results from objective self-evaluation. Coupled with other qualities, it produced great results in war and helped make Ike Eisenhower the ideal of effective democratic leadership to the American people. It is a facet of the practical, externalized Eisenhower mind.

But there remains the question how much of an asset this simple and direct aspect of the Eisenhower personality is in meeting problems outside his military experience.

As the new president of Columbia University, the General felt a certain diffidence in unaccustomed academic circles. According to reports, there were some on the Columbia faculty who did not at first regard him as the greatest of

Columbia presidents. There was the story of the question asked by one of the faculty assistants when Eisenhower took over, as to how he should be addressed: General or President? The reply, in effect, was, just call me Ike. It was a good reply in the terms of Ike Eisenhower's experience in the problem of welding different groups into a cooperative team. But it was a slightly false note in the dignified and formal surroundings of Columbia. It did not effectively answer the question. Ike, however, as always, quickly learned his job.

His qualities of simplicity, directness and clear thinking, which made impress on academicians and common folk alike, were summed up in an editorial in *The New York Times* on April 26, 1946, following his address to the newspaper publishers. It said: "One reason for General Eisenhower's steadily mounting prestige is his common-sense approach to difficult and intricate problems. A second reason is his ability to express the problem clearly. A third is his always evident sincerity."

These qualities of the practical, intelligent and well-meaning man undoubtedly explain much of the General's prestige. But deeper than that, in the conscious or unconscious attitude of the American people toward him, is the sense of his selfless devotion to duty and the moral standards in public life which his philosophy demands.

In this the symbolic Eisenhower and the practical person who is Eisenhower meet. Dwight Eisenhower has said that he has never been ambitious for place and power; his ambition has been to do his job well and eventually retire to private life. His achievement of place and power have been incidental to the performance of his duty as he has seen it. Only his sense of duty could deviate him from this plan.

He clearly considers high office as an opportunity to serve, to perform a duty to his people, rather than as a means of achieving personal ambitions. Indeed, as he wrote to Mr. Finder, only "some obvious and overriding reasons" would allow him to enter any public field other than that to which he has devoted most of his life. His attitude toward the power which a leader of democracy must assume is modeled after that of Lincoln. He described it in his address to the first Columbia College Forum February, 1949:

"I think that far more important than talking, possibly, about any living man today would be to think a little bit about the life of the man whose birthday falls today, Abraham Lincoln.

"I think each of you has a very special reason for venerating his memory. We think of him always as the great American. One thing I like to believe about him is this: that he had the proper attitude toward power. He finally came to be the President of the United States in a very special time, in war, when the power devolving upon the President of the United States is so great that if used evilly or to the disadvantage of his fellow citizens it can become a dictatorship. And that was especially true in the war between the States, because the very life of the nation was at stake day by day.

"Yet there is nothing in Lincoln's life or in Lincoln's writings that could lead any of us to believe that he recognized or believed that he himself was a source of power. He was a director of power, a man who might give it its trend to go somewhere, but he had no ambition to associate the source of power with himself, and, thereby, rule others. He served others. That, to me, is the true essence of liberty and of freedom.

"A man placed in a position where he could have been arbitrary, unjust, unfair, could have done many things for his self-glorification, and he refused to do any of them. As he said: 'I have been given a job to do for the United States. And I will serve in that job to the best of my ability. More I cannot do.' . . .

"Very naturally when we talk about a man so great, of such overwhelming stature, the thought comes to us: 'Well, what relationship has that got to us; we are no Lincolns?' But the principles by which he lived, the faith he had in freedom and liberty was exemplified, for example, in his very great and, I believe, it was called an unconstitutional act, in the Emancipation of the slaves. His passion for individual liberty of thought, of worship, freedom to act, freedom of opportunity, is the virtue that each of us can emulate and more than that, I believe, it is the virtue that each of us *must* emulate if we are to preserve to ourselves the opportunities which,

I believe, I recognized in my boyhood, and which I am certain that you young men see around you on every side."

One of his soldiers is said to have remarked that Eisenhower is as American as pumpkin pie. He is grass-roots American. Like Lincoln he is a completely self-made man. He knows the value of money because he has earned everything he has. He deeply shares in the qualities and characteristics that make Americans distinctive from other peoples. He knows intuitively the problems and hopes and possibilities of America. Moreover, he understands a great deal about the rest of the world through his tours of duty abroad.

He is accustomed to dealing with vast numbers of men and to handling immense material resources with wisdom and foresight. He has shown himself one of the most remarkable diplomats in the nation's history. If the key to his thinking is "cooperation," no one is more fitted to put that quality to use in solving the great problems of today. Before these problems he stands modestly unafraid, calmly confident that international cooperation is possible and real peace can be achieved for the benefit of mankind through the years to come.

Greater than his many competencies, and central to his ideas of freedom, initiative and self-reliance, is the kind of faith and moral character which are so badly needed by the confused Western world. There are signs that many Americans are beginning to revolt against the negativeness of a materialistic outlook that has stressed comfort-seeking and the acquisition of material things at a cost to spiritual satisfaction and real happiness. Thus it might be argued that Dwight Eisenhower's amazing hold on the imagination of millions is as much a response to his affirmative attitude on the true values of life as to his personal charm and great achievements.

One more quotation will suffice to complete this effort to record what Eisenhower thinks. It has to do with America's opportunity and future. It was said to his Columbia students in June, 1950.

"The United States of America has been marked to wear the burdensome but glorious mantle of world leadership. Today's great opportunity in this country is to make that leader-ship a moral, intellectual and material model for all time. I am glad the opportunity is in your hands."

This was spoken from the heart. It embodies in simple terms a fundamental faith and optimism which answers a pro-found need of the people of the United States and of other free nations.